# ONE ROOM SCHOOLS

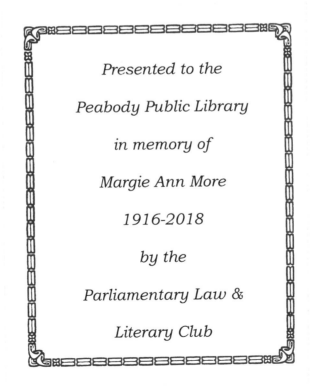
12/12/18

DISCARD

# ONE ROOM SCHOOLS

Stories from the Days of
1 Room, 1 Teacher, 8 Grades

## Susan Apps-Bodilly

Wisconsin Historical Society Press

Published by the Wisconsin Historical Society Press
*Publishers since 1855*

© 2013 by the State Historical Society of Wisconsin

For permission to reuse material from *One Room Schools,* (978-0-87020-615-3), please access www.copyright.com or contact the Copyright Clearance Center, Inc. (CCC), 222 Rosewood Drive, Danvers, MA 01923, 978-750-8400. CCC is a not-for-profit organization that provides licenses and registration for a variety of users.

**wisconsinhistory.org**

Photographs identified with WHi or WHS are from the Society's collections; address requests to reproduce these photos to the Visual Materials Archivist at the Wisconsin Historical Society, 816 State Street, Madison, WI 53706.

Cover photo: Reed School, a Wisconsin Historic Site in Neillsville. Photo by Mark Fay
Previous pages: Eleanora Witt, Jerry Apps's mother, also attended the Chain O' Lake School. She is standing in the back, under the globe. Collection of Susan Apps-Bodilly
Opposite page: Wild Rose Pioneer Museum. Photo by Steve Apps

Printed in the United States of America

Designed by Mayfly Design

22  21  20  19  18        2  3  4  5

Library of Congress Cataloging-in-Publication Data
Apps-Bodilly, Susan
  One room schools : stories from the days of 1 room, 1 teacher,
8 grades / Susan Apps-Bodilly.
      pages cm
  Includes index.
  ISBN 978-0-87020-615-3 (pbk. : alk. paper)  1.  Rural schools—Wisconsin.  I. Title.
  LB1567.B435 2013
  370.9173'409775—dc23
                                    2013007081

∞  The paper used in this publication meets the minimum requirements of the American National Standard for Information Sciences—Permanence of Paper for Printed Library Materials, ANSI Z39.48-1992.

*Dedicated to my parents, Jerry and Ruth Apps,*
*and to the teachers and students of Wisconsin's one-room schools.*
*I am so honored to share your stories with others.*

This is the inside of the Chain O' Lake School in 1945. Jerry Apps and his twin brothers, Donald and Darrel, were in the same classroom. Do you see the little sandbox on the left? Their teacher, Miss Thompson, used it for science lessons. Did you notice the piano? Who is pictured on the wall above the chalkboard? Using pictures and stories from the past, you can learn about the days when there was one schoolroom, one teacher, and 8 grades. **Courtesy of Jerry Apps**

# Contents

The Chain O' Lake School building and woodshed as it looked circa 1962. In the past, country students attended all 8 grades in a one-room school like this one. Today this former schoolhouse is a private home. **Photo by Jerry Apps**

# Chapter 1

## The First Day of School

It was the first day at the one-room Chain O' Lake School in central Wisconsin. In September 1939, Jerry Apps was 5 years old. He knew it was a special day because he wore a new pair of striped bib overalls and a new cotton shirt. "For the first time all summer, I had to comb my hair before putting on my hat and I hated that," Jerry remembers. He carried his lunch bucket and school supplies. The school supplies purchased at the Wild Rose Drug Store were 2 pencils and a Big Chief writing **tablet** that cost 5 cents. His father had sharpened the pencils with his jackknife.

**tablet** (**tab** lit): a pad of paper stuck together on one end and used for writing

This is a tablet of writing paper. On the first day of school, Jerry Apps brought a tablet like this one and 2 pencils to school. What supplies do you need for school? **Courtesy of Jerry Apps**

At 8:30 a.m., Jerry heard the schoolhouse bell ring. On a clear day you could hear it 2 miles away—it would echo down the valley and over the hills. He knew that this bell meant he had 30 minutes to get to school. He did not want to be late. If you were early, you had some time to play before school started.

When he went through the front gate of the schoolyard, many children were already there greeting each other. The Kolka boys had the longest walk—almost 2 miles. No students had to walk more than 2 miles to school.

The white schoolhouse was a rectangular wooden building with steps leading up to the front door. The bell tower holding the huge metal bell they had heard earlier was above the front door.

In the schoolyard, Jerry could see the flagpole in front of the school and the teeter-totter, or seesaw, was to his right. To the left of the school was the pump house. The pump house was not a house for people, but a small building that "housed" the hand-crank water pump.

The building with the pump was also used as a woodshed. Before the school year started, a school board member had chopped wood at his farm and delivered it to the shed. The shed was full of huge chunks of oak wood. The school used a woodstove for heat in cold weather.

On the left side of this building, there were some trees with space between each one. Jerry would soon learn that this area was the softball field. Along the fence on the left side of the schoolhouse was a row of lilac bushes.

Jerry walked into the school. Just inside the front door was a room with hooks to hang coats. Jerry's first teacher, Miss Piechowski, helped him find a place for his lunch bucket. The cloakroom had 2 doors leading into the classroom, one on the left and one on the right. Jerry could see the one room with desks for all 8 grades—first grade through eighth.

Do you see the water pump at the left of this photo taken outside of Eagle Corners School in Richland County? **WHi Image ID 97526**

These Chain O' Lake students are posing for a picture in 1943. Back to front: Nita Dudley, Geraldine Hudziak, Clair Jenks, Norman Hudziak, Jim Steinke, Jerry Apps, Jim Kolka, Dave Kolka, Mildred Swendryznski, Darrel Apps, and Donald Apps. **Courtesy of Jerry Apps**

Right away, Jerry noticed the unusual smell of the oiled wood floor. In August, Mrs. Jenks had been paid 5 dollars to come in and get the schoolroom ready. She lived a short distance away and was the mother of Clair, a third-grade boy. She washed all of the windows, dusted, and chased out the summer mice that were hiding in the corners. She used a sweeping compound, such as sawdust mixed with an oil, to gather up the dust and dirt from the wood floors. Many other folks in the neighborhood also helped get the school ready for students.

In some school communities, all the parents met at the school to clean and paint before the first day of classes. They made sure the buildings were ready and the water pump was working. They cut the weeds that had grown in the schoolyard over the summer. In this way, the school belonged to everyone.

An eighth-grade student pulled the long rope to ring the bell at 8:55. This meant 5 more minutes for the last **dawdler** to run to school. Then it was 9 o'clock. The first day of school had begun.

**dawdler** (**dawd** lur): someone who wastes time or takes a long time to do something

Students of different ages are working at their desks in a schoolroom in Grant County. What do you notice about the number of stars on the flag? **Image ID 66024**

# Chapter 2

## The One-Room Schoolhouse

In this chapter, you will think like a **historian**. Thinking like a historian means you can learn from the stories of people and events of the past. You will compare your school with one from the year 1939. Can you picture yourself walking into the one-room Chain O' Lake School, as Jerry did on his first day in 1939? Imagine a beautiful fall morning in central Wisconsin. The leaves are turning colors, there is a slight breeze, and you are walking to school. You woke up early and did your chores— fed the cows or gathered eggs from the chickens. You are excited to start school and meet new friends.

---

**historian** (hi **stor** ee uhn): someone who studies and tells or writes about the past

Students in Jerry's school were all together in one room. All grades from first through eighth grade learned from each other. Older students helped the younger ones, and the younger children watched and listened to the older students. There was no kindergarten. Children began school at age 5 or 6. One-room schools served all the school-age children in the surrounding neighborhood. There could be as many as 50 students in one school, including many sets of brothers and sisters. There always was only one teacher.

The Chain O' Lake School had a wire fence with a gate around the schoolyard. The building was a rectangular shape with the front door on the end facing the road.

In 1939, very few country schools had indoor plumbing. In opposite corners, near the back of the Chain O' Lake schoolyard, were the 2 outhouses. Do you know what an outhouse is? To go the bathroom, students went outside to the outhouse—even in winter and on rainy days.

The Chain O' Lake School had a building that was used as a woodshed and pump house. This pump was the school's source of water. In the shed there were enough small pieces of wood, or kindling, to start a fire in the school's woodstove, as well as a pile of oak wood to keep the fire going. This shed also stored rakes and shovels. A chore for older boys and girls was to take care of the schoolyard and rake leaves. In the winter, the teacher or the older students had to shovel snow off the steps and make a path to each outhouse.

There were 2 windows on either side of the schoolhouse door and many windows along each side to let in as much light as possible. In 1939, many schools did not yet have electricity. Inside, gas lamps

A teacher and her students pose for a photo in front of Fernside School in Sauk County in 1900. Do you see the outhouse in the schoolyard? **Courtesy of William Schuette**

hung from the ceiling on wire. They provided light on dark, cloudy days and for special evening programs.

After you walked up the Chain O' Lake School steps, you hung up your coat inside on a hook in the cloakroom. The cloakroom was a small hallway where all the coats, boots, hats, scarves, and lunches were stored during the day. Inside the one big schoolroom were many sizes of desks in rows facing the chalkboard. The smallest

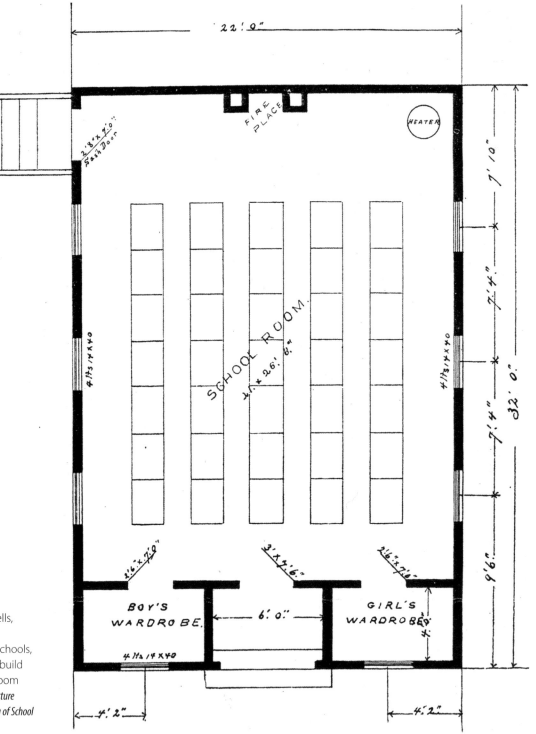

22' 0"

FIRE
PLACE

HEATER

2'8"x 7'0"
Sash Door

4 lts 14 x 40

SCHOOL ROOM.
24' x 26' 8"

4 lts 14 x 40

7' 10"

7' 4"

7' 4"

32' 0"

9' 6"

2'6"x 7'0"

3' x 4' 6"

2'6"x 7'0"

BOY'S
WARDROBE.

6' 0"

GIRL'S
WARDROBE

4 lts 14 x 40

4' 2"

4' 2"

In 1892, Oliver E. Wells, the Wisconsin state superintendent of schools, offered this plan to build and furnish a one-room schoolhouse. *Architecture Ventilation and Furnishing of School Houses, 1892*

desks for the littlest children were in the front of the room, while the oldest children sat in the back.

A Red Wing Pottery water cooler was at the back of the room. One student had the job of carrying a pail of water from the pump outside and filling up the gray porcelain water cooler. The water cooler had a little pipe that came out and curved up. When you pushed a button, the water bubbled up for a drink. Students did not have this kind of container for drinking water at home. At home, they kept water in a bucket and drank from a water dipper, which is a metal cup with a long handle. New first-grade students had to figure out how to use the button so the water would not splash in their faces! There was also a little sink for washing. The sink was a square shape with a drain in the bottom. A pipe carried the water from the drain and through the wall. The water dumped outside on the ground. In the winter, there was a pyramid of ice that formed on the ground under the drainpipe!

In the back of the room, a wood box stored the wood for the woodstove. Next to the woodstove was a large bookshelf with many books; this was the school "library." There was also a cupboard with the teacher's supplies, paper, and chalk.

At the front of the room was the teacher's desk. On the teacher's desk were the teacher's plans and books for every subject. There was also a large, battery-operated Philco radio for listening to educational radio programs. Next to the teacher's desk was a small table with chairs used for reading or math groups. Some schools had a wooden bench for children to sit on during small group activities.

Across the wall in the front of the room was a chalkboard. The teacher wrote the day's schedule and lessons for each grade on the

| Time Begun | No. minutes | Class or Grade | Subject | Time Begun | No. m |
|---|---|---|---|---|---|
| 9:00 | Opening | All | Exercise | 1:00 | 1 |
| 9:10 | 15 min | 7 + 8 | Arithmetic | 1:10 | 1 |
| 9:25 | 15 min | 1st | Reading | 1:20 | 1 |
| 9:40 | 10 min | 2nd | Reading | 1:35 | 1 |
| 9:50 | 15 min | 3rd + 4th | Reading | 1:45 | 1 |
| 10:05 | 15 min | 5th + 6th | Reading or History | 2:00 | 1 |
| 10:20 | 10 min | 8th | Physiology | 2:15 | 1 |
| 10:30 | 10 min | All | Recess | 2:30 | 15 |
| 10:45 | 15 min | 1st + 2nd | Language | 2:40 | 1 |
| 10:55 | 10 min | 7th + 8th | Grammar | 2:55 | 1 |
| 11:10 | 20 min | 3rd + 4th | Arithmetic | 3:05 | 10 |
| 11:30 | 15 min | 5th + 6th | Arithmetic | 3:20 | 1 |
| 11:45 | 15 min | 7th + 8th | History | 3:30 | 1 |
| 12:00 | 60 min | All | Lunch | 3:15 | 1 |
|  |  |  |  | 4:00 |  |

On this chalkboard at the Halfway Prairie School, located near Black Earth, is an example of a typical morning schedule in a one-room school. Can you see when you would have met in a group with the teacher?

|  |  |  |  |
|---|---|---|---|
| 1:00 | 10 min | 1st | Reading |
| 1:10 | 10 min | 2nd | Reading + Arith. |
| 1:20 | 10 min | 7th + 8th | Reading |
| 1:35 | 15 min | 3rd + 4th | Language |
| 1:45 | 10 min | All | Drawing |
| 2:00 | 15 min | 5th | Geography |
| 2:15 | 15 min | 6th + 7th | Geography |
| 2:30 | 15 min | All | Recess |
| 2:40 | 10 min | 1st | Reading |
| 2:55 | 15 min | 2nd | Spelling |
| 3:05 | 10 min | 3rd | Spelling |
| 3:20 | 15 min | 5th + 6th | Language |
| 3:30 | 10 min | 4th | Spelling |
| 3:40 | 5 min | 5th + 6th | Spelling |
| 3:45 | 15 min | 7th + 8th | Spelling or Agriculture |

The afternoon schedule is listed on this chalkboard. **Photos by Susan Apps-Bodilly**

chalkboard. Above this was a chart of cursive handwriting and a printed alphabet. On the wall in almost every one-room school were pictures of Presidents George Washington and Abraham Lincoln. Attached to the chalkboard was a set of maps that pulled up and down, like a window shade, showing all the continents of the world. In the front right corner of the room was a large upright piano.

Can you picture yourself walking into the school from 1939? Girls wore a skirt and blouse or a dress. They wore stockings and leather lace-up shoes. The boys wore denim overalls from the Sears, Roebuck & Co. catalog or blue jeans. They wore long-sleeved buttoned shirts with a collar. A boy wore shoes with laces to be tied and socks. Some boys had **suspenders** to keep their pants up.

In the winter, girls wore long, brown cotton stockings and the boys wore long underwear under their shirts and pants. Some boys liked to joke that a Wisconsin winter was so cold that they never took off their long underwear from the first snow to the last! Both boys and girls wore wool snow pants to keep warm while walking to school. Jerry's family bought boots at the Wild Rose Mercantile, which was a general store that sold everything from clothing to groceries. When he was young, snow boots had 4 buckles on the side. Jerry remembers, "When you were old enough for 6-buckle overshoes, you knew you were growing up!" Jerry had a winter coat made of water-resistant woolen cloth and a cap with earflaps made of real cat fur to keep his head warm on the walk to school. Children wore woolen mittens and scarves that their grandmothers made, perhaps as a Christmas gift. On the walk to school, children bundled

---

**suspenders** (suh **spen** durz): straps worn over a person's shoulders and attached to their pants to hold them up

# Thinking Like a Historian

Historic photographs contain evidence, or clues, about the past. Historians study these photographs for clues about what life used to be like.

These photographs are examples of what students wore to school in the 1930s and 1940s. Compare their clothes to the outfits you wear today. What do you notice about their clothing? How did the girls style their hair? What kinds of shoes do you see? What has changed? What has remained the same? What else can you learn from these photographs?

This is the 1939 class photo from Sunny View School in Green Lake County. Notice the girls' dresses and the boys' overalls. One boy is wearing suspenders. **Courtesy of Ruth Plautz**

This is the Winnebago County Stone School class and their teacher, Jennie Frees, in 1949. The author's aunt, Marcie Kirk, is in the front row, second from the right. **Courtesy of Marcie Kirk Apps**

up with only their eyes peeking out above a scarf. By the time they got to school, the scarf had frozen from breathing into it.

Grandmothers and mothers often made clothes "by hand" with a sewing machine. Few families could afford to buy all of their clothes

at a store. Mothers sewed patches over holes, mended socks, and reused clothes whenever possible.

Many **rural** families were very poor. Lily Wolff was a teacher at Wildwood School in Oneida County in 1944. She was a kind and caring teacher. She remembers a little girl named Esther in her class who did not have a winter coat. "She only had an old sweater with no buttons," recalls Miss Wolff. She worried that Esther would get frostbite walking to and from school. Miss Wolff asked her own mother to make a coat for Esther. Her mother used some extra fabric to sew a coat for Esther. Esther was so excited to have her own

The children of Coher School in Crawford County stand on a storm shelter in 1950. Some schools without a basement had a separate underground cellar. When the teacher saw dark clouds or when there were high winds, everyone would run into the shelter to be safe from the storm. **Courtesy of Ada McKnight**

**rural** (**rur** uhl): having to do with the countryside or farming

After a blizzard in 1909, a father brings his children home from school in a sleigh pulled by a horse.
Courtesy of Jean V. Christenson

winter coat. Every day when she got to school, she said, "Thank you for my teacher coat!"

Darlene Jacobson Ingrassia started school at age 5 in 1931 at the Union Valley School in Iowa County. Darlene's mother and Darlene's 5 aunts also attended the same school when they were children. Darlene wrote a letter to her granddaughter, Sarah, about her school memories. "Most of the time we walked to school, which was close to 2 miles from home," she wrote. "In bad weather, Dad would take us or we would have to stay home. We did not have a car. He would have to take us with our horse and buggy depending on the road conditions. Our life revolved around the school, the church, and the community." Darlene remembers her school even though it has been closed for many years. "My school is still there and has not been preserved. It makes me sad, as eventually it will be all gone. My family and I go there sometimes when we are in the area. They are all fascinated to see and learn about it—what memories! I can hardly believe the contrast between then and today's life. We all owe a lot to those teachers, our parents, and the Union Valley School."

What is the same about the one-room schoolroom compared to a schoolroom of today? What is different? Today in classrooms, students are usually all about the same age. In a school building, there are many classrooms, bathrooms, and drinking fountains. There may be a secretary and a principal working in the office. Schools have a cafeteria, gymnasium, computer lab, library, music room, art room, and playgrounds.

Many people who attended one-room schools have very accurate memories of the smells, sounds, and sights from their first school. They may have attended the same school for 8 years. You can find out about the past by asking questions and interviewing someone who lived during that time.

Learning about Wisconsin's one-room schools gives us a picture of life in an earlier time. With the stories from teachers and from the children who attended them, we learn about our history. How does learning about the past help us understand our lives today?

Whitewater State Normal School graduate Alice Holloway teaches her students at Bay Hill School in Williams Bay, in 1930. Her son Richard Quinney once said, "She kept a few photographs of her early students; they were among her most cherished possessions." WHi Image ID 101481

## Chapter 3

### The One-Room Teacher and the Community

C an you imagine being a teacher in a one-room school? In most cases, teachers were young women, sometimes only 19 or 20 years old. At first, it may seem like a lonely job. However, in 1939, Miss Piechowski had support from many people in the Chain O' Lake community.

Today, your teacher has to graduate from college to earn a diploma and a teaching **license**. In 1939, to become a teacher in a one-room school, a man or woman attended **normal school** for 2 years to earn a teaching certificate.

**license** (**lı** suhns): a document showing permission or approval from the government

**normal school** (**nor**-muhl skool): a 2-year school for training teachers

This photograph shows the exterior of the Vernon County Normal School in Viroqua. In a normal school, teachers received training to work in a one-room school. **WHi Image ID 55180**

Each county in Wisconsin had a **superintendent**. This person was **responsible** for all of the schools and teachers in their county. There could be more than 100 one-room schools in a county—this was too many for the superintendent to visit. A county supervising teacher came out to a school to watch a teacher and his or her teaching methods. If a teacher knew that the supervising teacher was coming, students knew to create a "good impression" because their teacher was being judged. However, the supervisor often came **unexpectedly**. After the visit, the supervisor

---

**superintendent** (soo pur in **ten** duhnt): the person in charge of a school system

**responsible** (ri **spon** suh buhl): having important duties, being in charge

**unexpectedly** (uhn ek **spek** tid lee): happening without warning

# Normal School, A School for Teachers

- 1848—Wisconsin becomes a state.
- 1849—The State Legislature makes a plan to create a school for teachers. However, there was little money for this plan.
- 1861—The office of county superintendent of schools is created.
- 1865—Laws are passed creating a system of Wisconsin normal schools for educating teachers.
- 1866—The first normal school opens in Platteville.
- 1899—Laws are passed allowing each county to have a normal school. There was a high demand for teachers at the time.

Here are the 1941 graduates of the Stevenson Training School. Later, it was renamed the Marinette Normal School. Three men and 30 women graduated on this day. **Courtesy of Shirley Bennett Madden**

133

John Swendrgynski                          TREASURER.

Chain O Lake School District No. 4                          Cr.

| DATE. | TO WHOM PAID. | NO. OF ORDER. | FUND. | ON WHAT ACCOUNT. | AMOUNT. |
|---|---|---|---|---|---|
| July 7. 1939 | Andrew Nelson | 1 | General | Auditing Books | 1.00 |
| July 7. 1939 | Winifred Davis | 2 | '' | '' '' '' | 1.00 |
| July 7. 1939 | Mrs. Anna La Page | 3 | '' | '' '' | 1.00 |
| July 28 1939 | F. Q. Compton & Co. | 4 | '' | Encyclopedias | 70.52 |
| July 28 1939 | MacKinley Jenks | 5 | '' | Broken Bones | 4.00 |
| Aug. 12 1939 | Arlin Handrich | 6 | '' | Wood | 20.00 |
| Aug. 18 1939 | Mrs. Mac. Jenks | 7 | '' | Cleaning School | 5.00 |
| Aug 18 1939 | Mackinley Jenks | 8 | '' | Labor on Toilets cutting Kindling | 11.00 |
| Aug 18 1939 | John Swendrgynsk. | 9 | '' | Labor on out Houses | 8.10 |
| Aug 19 1939 | Arlin Handrich | 10 | '' | Wood | 20.00 |
| Aug 18 1939 | Jesse DeWitt | 11 | '' | Cleaning Houses | 6.00 |
| Aug 18 1939 | R. K. Hotz | 12 | '' | Building Material | 7.07 |
| Aug 18 1939 | Wild Rose Lumber Co. | 13 | '' | Building Material | 30.44 |
| Sept 13 1939 | Theresa Piechowski | 14 | '' | 1st Month Salary | 85.00 |
| Sept 28 1939 | Miss Piechowski | 15 | '' | ½ of Second Month | 42.50 |
| Oct 19 1939 | T. W. Stevens Co. | 16 | '' | School Supplies | 24.76 |
| Oct 19 1939 | O. E. Williams | 17 | '' | Insurance | 4.25 |
| Oct 19 1939 | Jesse De Witt | 18 | '' | Convention | 5.05 |
| Oct 19 1939 | Arlin Handrich | 19 | '' | '' '' | 5.05 |
| Oct 19 1939 | Miss Piechowski | 20 | '' | last half of 2 month | 42.50 |

This is a page from the Chain O' Lake School treasurer's book from 1939. On September 13, Miss Piechowski was paid her first month's salary. **Courtesy of Jerry Apps**

reported back to the superintendent about the ability of the teacher in each one-room school.

There were many **expectations** for one-room teachers. Parents expected the teacher to be a role model of appropriate behavior for the students. A female teacher wore nice clothes, such as a blouse with a long skirt or a long dress, every day. There was a rule that female teachers could not get married—if they did, they often left the job. Back then, most married women wanted to stay home with their own families. In later years, some one-room schoolteachers could marry and continue teaching.

In September 1939, Miss Piechowski earned 85 dollars for her first month's salary. For 9 months of teaching, she earned 765 dollars. In 1939, a loaf of bread cost 10 cents. Do you know how much it costs to buy a loaf of bread today? Some teachers gave money back to their parents to help their family.

Teachers often lived with a family from the school. It was part of a teacher's contract that a place to live would be provided for her. The teacher often did not pay rent for the room or for food. This is called giving the teacher "room and board." The room was plain as plain could be—often there was only a bed and a dresser.

Lily Wolff was a teacher at Wildwood School in northern Wisconsin. Here she is as a 19-year-old teacher shoveling snow.
Courtesy of Lily P. Kongslien

---

expectation (ek spek **tay** shun): an idea or belief about what should happen

# Rules of Conduct for Rural Teachers

Here is an example of some **requirements** for a teacher who worked in a one-room school. This list is from a handout offered to visitors at the Rhinelander School Museum at the Pioneer Park Historical Complex.

1.  Teachers must have legal **qualifications**.
2.  They must keep the schoolroom neat and clean.
3.  Sweep the floor at least once daily and clean the blackboards each day.
4.  Ring the school bell promptly at 9 o'clock.
5.  Start the fire early enough to have the room warm by 9 a.m.
6.  Drinkable water must be available in the building each day.
7.  Keep the school in session until 4 p.m.
8.  Prepare and present a Christmas program for the community.
9.  **Observe** Arbor Day, to beautify the school grounds.
10. Women teachers may not dress in bright colors.
11. Dresses must be of appropriate length.
12. Married teachers will not be hired.
13. Teachers who engage in **unseemly** conduct will be dismissed.
14. The teacher's instruction must prepare the 8th grade students to pass the county examination, which will qualify them for high school entrance.

---

**requirement** (ri **kwɪr** muhnt): something that you have to do

**qualification** (kwahl uh fuh **kay** shuhn): a skill that makes you able to do a task

**observe** (uhb **zurv**): celebrate a holiday

**unseemly** (uhn **seem** lee): not in good taste or judgment

In 1939, many Wisconsin farmhouses did not yet have electricity or indoor plumbing. The teacher had a washbowl and a pitcher in the bedroom to use for washing. She used the family's outhouse behind the house for a bathroom. The teacher had to walk to school in the morning before the students. She stayed after school ended to work on lessons and then walked home. The teacher ate meals as a member of the family during the week. On the weekends, some teachers traveled home to stay with his or her family.

In some school districts, the families shared the living arrangements for the teacher. The teacher moved from farm to farm during the school year. She or he spent one to 2 weeks living in a room at the home of each family.

When Jerry Apps was 3 years old, a teacher lived at his house. Her name was Vera Bartsch. Miss Bartsch became good friends with his family. She ate with the family and often played with the children in the evenings. She even met her husband when she lived at Jerry's house! She married Donnie Davies, who lived on the next farm. Because she got married, she stopped teaching. Miss Bartsch remained good friends with the family for many years. Would you like to have your teacher live in a room at your house?

Today, your school district has a group of community members that, along with the superintendent, makes decisions about your school. Some have children in the school and others do not. School board **candidates** "run" for the position. There are elections to vote for school board members.

---

**candidate** (**kan** duh dayt): someone running for office in an election

157

# Herman Apps    TREASURER.

Chain O Lake    School District No. 4    Cr.

| DATE. | TO WHOM PAID. | NO. OF ORDER. | FUND. | ON WHAT ACCOUNT. | AMOUNT. | |
|---|---|---|---|---|---|---|
| July 3 45 | Collector of State | 1 | General | withholding tax | 14. | 60 |
| July 6 1945 | Mackinly Genks | 2 | " | Auditing Books | 1. | 00 |
| July 6 1945 | Robert John | 3 | " | Auditing Books | 1. | 00 |
| July 6 1945 | Vilas Olson | 4 | " | Auditing Books | 1. | 00 |
| Aug 17 1945 | Mrs Gust Hudziak | 5 | " | Cleaning Schoolhouse | 7. | 37 |
| Aug 30 1945 | G. M. Dopp | 6 | " | Wind Insurance | 21. | 60 |
| Sept 14 1945 | Maxine Thompson | 7 | " | 1st month salary | 125. | 00 |
| Sept 15 1945 | Dilts & Son | 8 | " | For Stove | 28. | 00 |
| Sept 15 1945 | Jessie Dewitt | 9 | " | Transportation fuel | 2. | 00 |
| Oct 9 1945 | J W Timm | 10 | " | Fire Insurance | 4. | 07 |
| Oct 9 1945 | Maxine Thompson | 11 | " | ½ of 2nd month Salary | 62. | 50 |
| Oct 9 1945 | Collector Int Rev. | 12 | " | withholding tax | 16. | 40 |
| Oct 11 1945 | Jessie Dewitt | 13 | " | Convention | 5. | 40 |
| Oct 11 1945 | Arlin Hendrich | 14 | " | Convention | 5. | 40 |
| Oct 30 1945 | Maxine Thompson | 15 | " | Last half of 2nd month Salary | 46. | 10 |
| Oct 30 1945 | Mrs Willie Miller | 16 | " | Cleaning school house | 7. | 37 |
| Nov 1 1945 | Jessie Dewitt | 17 | " | Kindling wood I cord | 13. | 00 |
| Nov 30 1945 | Maxine Thompson | 18 | " | 3rd month Salary | 125. | 00 |
| Nov 20 1945 | Milwaukee Sentinel | 19 | " | Paper for school | 4. | 00 |

In 1945, Herman Apps, Jerry's father, was the Chain O' Lake School treasurer. Maxine Thompson was the teacher. Her salary was $125.00 a month. What other things were paid for in the fall of 1945? **Courtesy of Jerry Apps**

In 1939, each school also had a school board. The school board members were elected; however, they had to be parents of children in the school. There was a president, a secretary, and a treasurer. For 5 dollars a year, the president was in charge of parent meetings. The secretary took notes at the meetings and earned 10 dollars a year. The treasurer had an important job. He had to write down and keep track of every dollar spent for the school in a treasurer's book.

When a school needed a new teacher, the school board worked with the county superintendent's office. The superintendent told the school board members about teachers who were ready for the job. The parents on the school board interviewed 3 teachers. They then decided who to hire to teach at their school. They could also fire a teacher if they knew she or he was not doing the job well.

In 1943, Jerry was 9 years old and going to the Chain O' Lake School. His little twin brothers were in first grade. The teacher was supposed to be teaching them to read. Their mother noticed that they were not learning as they should be. According to the treasurer's book for the school, the teacher did not stay a full year. Her last month's salary was in February. The school board hired a new teacher to finish the year.

The school board determined how much to pay a teacher, and she received her paycheck from them. Members of the school board were also responsible for keeping the school building and schoolyard in good condition. The buildings had to meet a certain standard set by the county. The school board members had a lot of responsibility and took it very seriously.

Clair Jenks's family lived less than a quarter mile from the Chain O' Lake School. There was a path through the woods between his

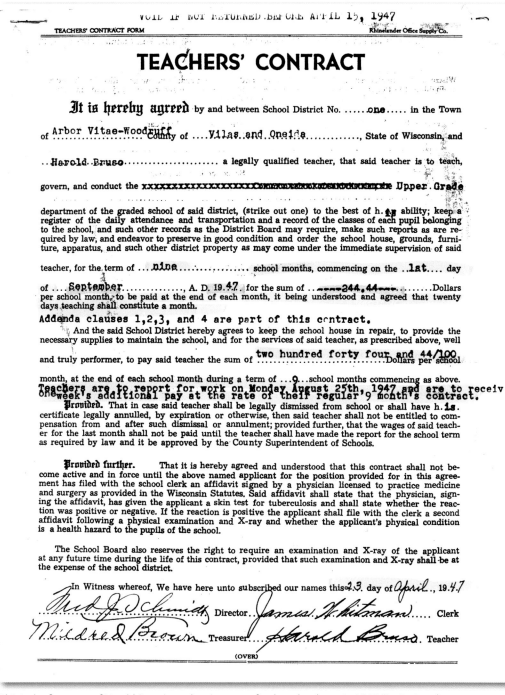

This is the first page of Harold Bruso's teachers' contract for the school year in 1947. By signing the contract, he agreed to teach in the town of Arbor Vitae-Woodruff. He would teach "to the best of his ability" and earn $244.44 a month. **Courtesy of Jerry Apps**

# The School Board

The parents on the school board did many jobs to keep the one-room school running smoothly. The members of the school board kept track of the money for the school and helped decide what to purchase for the school.

Here are some of the entries from the Chain O' Lake School treasurer's book listing things bought for the 1939 to 1940 school year:

- July 28, Purchase encyclopedias: $70.52
- August 12, Wood: $20.00
- August 18, Wild Rose Lumber, building supplies: $30.44
- October 19, School supplies: $24.76
- April 16, Kerosene: $2.95
- April 25, School supplies: $12.00

house and the school. Since the Jenkses lived close to school, Clair's father could walk over and start the wood stove on cold mornings. Mr. Jenks earned 11 dollars during the winter for building the fires.

A few times during the year, Mrs. Jenks cleaned the school. On Saturday, October 28, the account book states that Mrs. Jenks was paid 4 dollars for her work. Can you guess why she cleaned the school in October? The reason was that the school closed for 2 weeks for what was called a "potato vacation." However, children did not go on a trip. In Waushara County, where the Chain O' Lake School was located, many families grew potatoes on their farms.

The students worked at home for the 2 weeks, picking potatoes or helping with the harvest.

The potato field at Jerry Apps's Waushara County farm was 20 acres. It took the full 2 weeks to harvest all of the potatoes. His family did all of the work "by hand," without machines. In the morning, they set out 50 potato boxes spaced apart in the field. Jerry's father and a hired man dug up each hill of potatoes with a 6-tined pitchfork. The children walked along, picked up the potatoes, and put them in a 5-gallon bucket. When the bucket was full, they poured the potatoes into a box. At noon, they hauled the full boxes to the house in a wagon pulled by horses. They stored the potatoes in the cellar for the winter. These potatoes would be sold in the spring. After a lunch break, they went back to the field and kept harvesting potatoes.

In 1939, the one-room Chain O' Lake School closed from Monday, October 16, to Friday, October 27, for the potato vacation. The teacher also went home and harvested potatoes with her family. Mrs. Jenks came in on Saturday and swept and dusted the empty school. It would be ready when Miss Piechowski and her students returned on Monday.

The people who lived in the Chain O' Lake community supported their school by helping in many ways. The teacher also understood that the children needed to work with their parents at home during harvest time in the fall, so the school closed. When it opened again, the teacher and students were ready to return to schoolwork.

This teacher is pulling the long rope to ring the school bell. At some rural schools, teachers and older students shared this responsibility. **WHi Image ID 83236**

Students and their teacher gather with a large American flag outside the Danz School, in the town of Berry in Dane County, 1921.
WHi Image ID 89545

# Chapter 4

## Duties and Responsibilities

**D**o you and your classmates share classroom jobs in your school? Students in the one-room school had duties, or jobs. Along with learning school subjects, students learned to be responsible and dependable. The rural community they lived in valued hard work.

Before coming to school in the morning, Jerry woke up early and did chores at home. Boys and girls who lived on a farm had to feed oats and corn to the chickens, gather eggs, or carry in wood for the kitchen woodstove. They might feed the calves or cats in the barn. When they arrived at school, there were more duties.

It was the job of the oldest students to raise the flag up the flagpole each day. Putting up the flag was the duty with the highest honor. There are specific rules for raising, lowering, folding, and storing a flag. The United States flag cannot touch the ground. If it does, this shows disrespect to our country. To raise the flag, one student pulled the rope to move the flag up the pole. Another student was careful to make sure the flag did not touch the ground. If it did, the student was **demoted** to a less important job. Each day, the whole school gathered outside near the flagpole to say the Pledge of Allegiance. With their right hand over their heart, the students and teacher would say: "I pledge allegiance to the Flag of the United States of America and to the Republic for which it stands, One Nation indivisible, with liberty and justice for all." ("Under God" was not added to the pledge until 1954.)

Students felt special when the teacher assigned them responsibilities to make the classroom run smoothly. The duties matched the age and ability of each child. When he was a first grader, Jerry's duty was to take the chalkboard erasers outside and beat them together to get the chalk dust out. Another job for the youngest students was emptying the wastebasket of paper and piling it neatly in a box next to the wood stove. The teacher would put the paper in the stove and light it to start the wood burning. One student might walk out to the road, open the mailbox, and get the mail each day. Other duties were straightening the bookshelf and putting supplies away. Younger students felt proud when they could help the teacher and their older classmates.

An older boy, such as Clair Jenks, had to pump water in the pump house. Then he carried the water in and poured it into the Red Wing

---

**demoted** (di **moh** tid): sent down to a lower job or rank

Pottery water cooler. This would be the school's drinking water for the day. Remember, in 1939, the schoolhouse did not have indoor plumbing or running water.

In 1939, Geraldine Hudziak, an older girl in Jerry's class, was responsible for sweeping cobwebs and dust out of the outhouses. That winter, Jim Steinke and other older students took turns shoveling snow paths from the school to the outhouses and the woodshed. Beginning in sixth grade, the strongest students were assigned the duty of carrying in the heavy pieces of oak wood for the stove. Ringing the bell to start the school day was a fun privilege for the oldest students. To ring the bell, an older student pulled on a big, fat rope that hung down into the cloakroom where the lunch boxes were stored. The rope was attached to the large bell that hung in the school's bell tower.

Another duty for eighth graders was serving on the safety patrol. Schools in Wisconsin received a kit with badges, a belt with a shoulder strap, and instructions. An older student became the captain of the safety patrol, another was a lieutenant, and others were patrol officers. The Chain O' Lake School was on a dirt road with very little traffic. Sometimes only 3 cars a day went past the school! Even so, students on the safety patrol **assisted** other children as they crossed the road.

One student's duty was to fill the Red Wing Pottery water cooler with water every day. The little bowl in front is where the water bubbles up to drink. You can see this at the Reed School historic site in Neillsville.
**Wisconsin Historical Society**

**assist** (uh **sist**): to provide help

These older students participated in a safety patrol training class at a Rock County school in 1950.
WHi Image ID 41158

One of the most important duties in the school was helping other students. All students were responsible for the education of everyone else at school. Older students often were the teacher's helpers. They assisted younger children with their lessons in reading and arithmetic. In this way, the younger students had many "teachers" to help them.

Today, most schools have a custodian to clean the school after students leave. The one-room schoolhouse did not have a person to come in and clean every day. The teacher depended on the students to help keep the room organized and clean. At the end of the day, students completed the clean-up chores of taking down the flag and washing the blackboards. If you did not do your duty well, you were moved back to a lower-level duty. If you did your duties well, you earned the honor of moving up to a duty with more responsibility.

When a student misbehaved at school, a teacher might require that child to stay after school. A consequence might be to do more duties or finish classroom work. The teacher could require the naughty student to write on the blackboard and fill it up with sentences such as "I will not pull Mildred Swendryznski's pigtails."

Miss Wolff, the former one-room school teacher from Oneida County, remembers, "There was a boy who was prone to whispering and talking during lessons. He also threw spit wads at a girl one row over. This was more than a little troublesome for me. I would never make a spectacle out of a student in front of the others. I am sure he had to sit in the coat hall for a while. I remember hearing that his brother ran home to tattle on him and tell his parents."

At the one-room school, your brothers and sisters were there with you. If you misbehaved, your parents knew right away that something had happened at school that day. In addition, you would be late to start your afternoon chores. Mother and Father would not be happy if you were late to help with the animals in the barn or supper in the kitchen! "When you were in trouble in school, you were in double trouble at home!" Miss Wolff says.

After supper, students did their homework before going to bed. Working hard, doing well in school, and learning to be responsible were important to the families of the one-room school community.

Indian children and adults pose outside of a one-room schoolhouse, likely near Hayward. Many of them have a book in their hands.
WHi Image ID 55936

# Chapter 5

# Reading Lessons

**D**id you know that learning to read helps you succeed in science, social studies, and every subject? Reading was as important for children in the one-room schools as it is for you today.

Jerry and Norman Hudziak were first graders at the Chain O' Lake School in 1939. Jerry remembers that Miss Piechowski had a fun way for them to learn words. She laid out a strip of paper and divided it into squares. In each square, she wrote words that Jerry and Norman needed to learn that day. She called the paper a "reading highway." Miss Piechowski gave Jerry a little red car and Norman a little green car. The boys took turns "driving" the cars down the paper

WISCONSIN YOUNG PEOPLE'S READING CIRCLE
PRIMARY CERTIFICATE
for the school year *1939-40*

This certifies that *Jerold Apps*, a pupil in *1st* Grade, *Chain O' Lakes* School, *Wild Rose*, Wisconsin, has satisfactorily read the following books, which are on the list of books of the Wisconsin Young People's Reading Circle for the school year above named, and is therefore entitled to this TESTIMONIAL of MERIT.

Title of Book
*Animal Book*
*The Story of Milk*
*The Wise Little Hen*
*Story of Buttons*
*School Days Here + There*

Title of Book
*Mrs. Collie and Her Two Little Puppies*

Note-If more books have been read, write their titles on the back of this certificate

Given at *Wautoma*, Wisconsin, this *19th* day of *April*, 19*40*

*Theresa Piechowski*
Teacher

*Arthur Dietz*
Principal or Superintendent

At the end of first grade, Jerry Apps received this award for his reading work.
Courtesy of Jerry Apps

highway. As they drove, they had to read the words in each box. They could help each other and teach each other the words. If they knew the word, they drove down the highway to the next word. Jerry did not have any little metal cars like this at home, so he thought this was a great way to learn. The boys kept driving their cars, learning and talking about all of the words.

After 6 weeks, the highway was very long and they knew many words! Soon, they were able to read and understand many stories. Jerry's first-grade "Wisconsin Young People's Reading Circle—Primary Certificate" lists the names of the books he completed as a first grader: *Animal Book*, *The Story of Milk*, *The Wise Little Hen*, *Story of Buttons*, *School Days Here & There*, and *Mrs. Collie and Her Two Little Puppies.*

The Chain O' Lake children learned the alphabet letters and the sounds of the letters. They wrote words with letters in "word families" to make rhymes. Some word families are the "at family"— cat, mat, sat, rat—and the "et family"—bet, get, let, met, net. Students in the one-room school met with the teacher in groups by reading level. Some groups had children of different ages. Students read out of "readers," which were books that included many short stories, poems, word lists, and assignments all in one book. The content of the stories and the vocabulary in each reader became more difficult for each grade level. These hardcover books had beautiful color pictures. Families often had to buy the books, so children took special care of them.

"I can not see any gold
in dandelion leaves," said John.
"The leaves look green to me."
"I wash them and cook them,"
said the little old lady.
"Then I eat them for my dinner."
"Are they good?" asked John.
"They are as good as gold,"
said the little old lady.
"In the grass they are weeds.
In the kettle they are gold."
105

A colorful picture from "The Dandelion Lady," a story in the science reader called *Outdoor Land*. Do you think dandelions are weeds or gold? *The Nature Activity Readers, Book One: Outdoor Land,* 1934

While the teacher was with one group, the other students worked at their desks on assignments such as penmanship (handwriting), spelling, grammar, or silent reading. The rule for this time of day was "work independently and quietly." Twins Donald and Darrel Apps remember that their teacher, Miss Thompson, told them the room had to be quiet enough to hear the tick tock of the wind-up clock hanging in the front of the room. Can you imagine how quiet the room was?

Lily Wolff, the teacher from Oneida County, remembers she had to be very organized. She wrote out detailed plans and "kept her eye on the clock" as she taught to make sure she fit in all of the lessons. Reading was usually at the beginning of the morning and again after lunch. Each reading group lesson was about 15 minutes. Students came to the front of the room to sit on little chairs in a circle or at a table. Each lesson was a review of the reading from the day before, followed by a new story and new vocabulary. Students also had to **recite** passages or poems from their books. Then, Miss Wolff would assign a "healthy, big, and good assignment" that was related to the readings of the day. She also expected her students to work quietly. She remembers telling them, "If you need to raise your hand to interrupt important reading group work, it better be worthwhile!"

If students finished their assignments during reading time, they could read books from the library bookcase. The Wildwood School where Miss Wolff taught also had a collection of rubber stamps with words on them. Students could press the wooden stamps into an inkpad and then onto a piece of paper, forming sentences.

What did students read in 1939? In *Elson-Gray Basic Readers: Book Two*, the stories listed are in categories: Boys and Girls, Out of Doors, Just for Fun, Big and Little Workers, Old Tales, Brave and True Stories, and Happy Day Stories. The stories included fairy tales, holiday stories, animal stories, folk tales, and poems. Do second-grade students read stories like these today?

Older children might have read from a book like *Fact and Story Readers: Book Five*. This book encouraged fifth-grade students to read about people from other places. The book has stories written about many different topics, such as the North Pole, George

---

**recite** (ri **sɪt**): say something aloud that you have memorized

This is a rubber stamp set with words like the one Miss Wolff had at the Wildwood School. **Photo by Susan Apps-Bodilly**

Washington, the Olympic Games, Robinson Crusoe, bees, planting trees, and explorers. The book also includes some famous fiction stories. Many of the authors of these stories are still popular to read today, including Mark Twain, Charles Dickens, and Leo Tolstoy. At the end of each story, there is a section of assignments. There are 5 or 6 questions that are "answered in the story" and another set of questions called "Thinking for Ourselves." Next are "Words and Phrases" to learn. Each story ends with a list of "Books to Enjoy," which are suggestions of more reading on the same subject. Some schools gave out a special certificate to each student who read a certain number of books in a year.

# Poetry

Many adults who attended one-room schools can still recite poems that they learned years ago as children.

A popular poem that many Wisconsin students learned was "The Village Blacksmith," by Henry Wadsworth Longfellow. It was originally published in 1841. This is the first stanza of the poem:

*Under a spreading chestnut-tree*
*The village smithy stands;*
*The smith, a mighty man is he,*
*With large and sinewy hands;*
*And the muscles of his brawny arms*
*Are strong as iron bands.*

A poem that the teacher might have assigned to younger students to memorize was "The North Wind," by Rebecca Foresman.

**The North Wind**

*"The north wind is cold,"*
*The robins say;*
*"And that is why robins*
*Must fly away."*

*"The north wind is cold*
*And brings the snow,"*

*Says Jenny Wren,*
*"And I must go."*

*"The north wind is cold*
*As cold can be,*
*But I'm not afraid,"*
*Says the chickadee.*

*So the chickadee stays*
*And sees the snow,*
*And likes to hear*
*The north wind blow.*

This poem is from *Elson-Gray Basic Readers: Book Two*, published in 1931 by Scott, Foresman and Company.

For one-room school students, reading lessons were an important part of each day. Reading your book, preparing for **recitation**, answering questions about the reading, and talking about the stories showed the teacher you were making progress as a reader. Miss Wolff encouraged younger students to "listen in" to the older students when they recited aloud in their groups. Older students could relearn lessons from the younger children while listening in on their lessons. Miss Wolff says, "This was an important way to learn from each other—it was like a big family learning together."

**recitation** (res i **tay** shuhn): a speech that is memorized and performed

Children play while their teacher watches from the porch, 1939. This one-room school is located in Grant County, south of Boscobel. WHi Image ID 24502

# Chapter 6

## Recess

**W**hat is your favorite part of the school day? Did you answer recess? Recess has changed little over the years. During recess you can stretch your legs, go outside, and get some fresh air to escape a stuffy schoolroom.

Country children did not have neighbors living next door. Their closest neighbor might have been miles away. They did not see their friends after school, so time with friends at recess was especially fun. Each school day had 2 recesses—one in the morning and one in the afternoon—which lasted about 15 minutes. After eating lunch, students also had playtime outside. Everyone enjoyed talking, laughing, and just being loud.

This is the same building, seen on pages 48–49, in 2010. Today it is a private home. What things are still the same? Do you notice the school bell in the tower behind the chimney? **Photo by Susan Apps-Bodilly**

No matter what the season of the year, children played games outside. During Jerry's first year of school, he remembers learning the rules for many games from the older students. The teacher usually did not come out for recess. The oldest children were in charge of the younger ones. Popular games at one-room schools included Drop the Handkerchief, Anti-I-Over, Kick the Can, Ring Around the Rosie, and London Bridge. On rainy days, children played games inside like Button, Button, Who's Got the Button?

Recess in the winter included many activities. A popular winter game called Fox and Geese was played on freshly fallen snow. To play this game of tag, children first walked around to create a round snow track that looked like a wheel with spokes. They then played tag on this snow path. Other times friends chose sides for snowball fights. They also built snow forts and snowmen and fell backward into the snow to make snow angels. On the hill near the schoolyard, Jerry and his friends skied down on their wooden skis. To put them on, you slid your regular boot into the leather strap. Children also raced down hills on sleds and toboggans. Darrel Apps remembers that his friend Jim Kolka had the best sled. It was a wooden Flexible Flyer sled with steel runners. It was the fastest sled and went farther than anyone else's.

Top: Students enjoy recess at the Pershing School in Baileys Harbor, spring 1947. Bottom: What games do you think these children are playing? **Collection of Ruby Schultz**

As soon as the winter snow melted and the muddy grass dried, the students at the one-room schools began the softball season. The shape of the softball diamond and the bases depended on each schoolyard's open areas and trees. At the Chain O' Lake School, first base was a box elder tree, second base was a black oak tree, and third base was a white oak tree. The field was not flat. You ran uphill to first base, uphill to second base, and downhill to third base and

Playing softball at Chain O' Lake School during recess was fun for all ages of children. Jim Kolka is batting and his brother Dave is the umpire. **Courtesy of Jerry Apps**

home. The wooden privacy wall for the boy's outhouse served as the backstop for home plate. A hard-hit ball often got stuck up in a tree. The fielder waited for the ball to drop down to catch the out.

Nearly everyone enjoyed playing softball at recess. It was more important to have fun than to win. The softball captains were the oldest students. They organized the softball game. All ages and both boys and girls played. Even the little first graders played along with the oldest eighth graders. The pitcher adjusted the throw according to the age of the batter. The team practiced during every recess and sometimes the teacher joined the game.

Teachers from neighboring schools often knew each other. They planned friendly softball competitions between schools. When Chain O' Lake School students traveled to the neighboring Dopp School to play a game, they had to be careful. The Dopp softball field was in a cow pasture! Fielders had to avoid stepping in cow pies during a game. Do you know what cow pies are?

The softball field at Ruth Olson's South Natwick School in Vernon County was different from Jerry's softball field. This one was on a steep hill. This area of Wisconsin has rolling hills and valleys. Pieces of wood served as the bases. Tall pine trees lined one edge of the softball field, and a fence lined the back of the field. A ball hit over this fence was a home run. Just like at Jerry's school, older

children taught the younger ones how to hold the bat, throw, and catch a ball. Softball taught the students more than how to play a game; it taught them **cooperation**.

Ruth remembers her sixth and seventh grade years when Mr. Robert Erickson was her teacher. This was the first time she had a man for a teacher in her one-room school. Mr. Erickson taught everyone how to play sports. He nailed a basketball hoop to the back of the school building and taught them the rules. He also taught them how to play football. One day, everyone was so involved in a

The children from the Dopp School in Portage County played softball against the students at Chain O' Lake School. Evelyn Kolka is the teacher in this picture from 1945. **Courtesy of Jerry Apps**

---

**cooperation** (koh op uh **ray** shuhn): working together to reach a goal

In 1937, Lloyd Fox was the teacher at Union No. 1 School in Pierce County. However, most one-room school teachers were women. **Courtesy of Edna Runquist**

game of football that they lost track of the time! At 1:30, they were still outside playing—a half hour after recess should have ended! Mr. Jacobson, a neighbor, drove by the school on his way to town. He called out angrily, "Do you know what time it is? Shouldn't you be inside teaching these children?" The embarrassed Mr. Erickson quickly sent everyone back inside. Do you think this teacher enjoyed recess as much as his students did?

What other activities did children do during recess? In some schoolyards, children played on a teeter-totter, or seesaw; a metal merry-go-round; or on the swings. However, most rural Wisconsin schools in 1939 did not have playground equipment.

Sometimes, children made up games of their own. Ruth remembers playing in the woods down below the school. "We all would climb the trees, make forts, and pretend things," Ruth says. "We had great imaginations—we pretended we were Tarzan, swinging in the trees."

These upper-grade students from the South Natwick School in Vernon County dressed warmly to go outside for recess in the winter of 1948. Did you notice the sled leaning against the steps? Do you see the buckle boots? Ruth Olson is number 12. **Courtesy of Ruth Olson Apps**

Marilyn Hanson went to the Pine River School in Leon Township in Waushara County. In the spring, the river would flood because of the melting snow. At that time of year she wore tall rubber boots over her shoes to keep them dry. At recess, she could not resist wading into the water. She loved walking in the water and did not mind when it went rushing into her boots! However, her teacher was not happy when she came in with a dripping-wet dress and had to take off her wet stockings. Marilyn had to hang them up to dry in the classroom on a wooden drying rack near the stove.

Beyond having fun, students learned many things during recess. Older children watched over the younger ones and taught them the game rules. When boys and girls of all ages played together, everyone learned patience and teamwork. At the one-room school, both the boys and the girls ran, played, and roamed together until they heard the bell signaling that recess was over.

This one-room school desk at the Wild Rose Pioneer Museum has an arithmetic book and a newspaper on it. Do you know what the hole in the desk was for? **Photo by Steve Apps**

# Chapter 7

## Lessons Learned

What subjects do you study in school? Students who attended the Chain O' Lake School carried home a report card every 9 weeks for their parents to sign. In 1939, Jerry's first-grade report card included these subject areas: Reading, Silent Reading, Language and Phonics, Spelling, Writing, Arithmetic, Geography, Grammar, Physiology, History, Civics, Drawing, Art, Agriculture, Music, and Physical Training.

Parents in the rural community felt that getting an education was an important way to become a better **citizen**. A quote from Abraham

**citizen** (**sit** uh zuhn): member of a particular country who has the right to live there

# Report Cards

When learning about the past, it is fun to study real things, or primary sources. A primary source is something that gives evidence from, or clues about, the past. Things like a photograph, a historic map, or an old letter or journal provide us with real information about the past. Some primary sources are not in writing but are actual items that were used in earlier times, like an old school book, clothing, a tool, and even a report card.

This is a picture of Jerry's first-grade report card. What do you notice about his first year at the one-room schoolhouse? Miss Piechowski did not give Jerry grades for all subjects, even though he was in the room for all of the subjects with the older students. He received grades for Reading, Language and Phonics, and Silent Reading. This is evidence that learning to read was the most important subject. What else do you notice? Was Jerry tardy to school? Was he absent during his first-grade year? Do you keep your report cards?

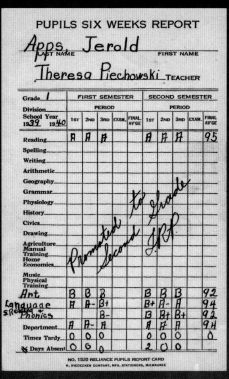

This is the front of Jerry's report card from first grade. He was never tardy! **Courtesy of Jerry Apps**

Lincoln on Jerry's fourth-grade report card in 1942 states, "I view education as the most important subject we as a people can be engaged in."

Do you enjoy learning to spell words? Each Monday morning in 1939, Miss Piechowski wrote lists of words for each grade on the blackboard. On Friday, there was a test. The little blue book called *The New National Speller,* published in 1926 by Row, Peterson and Company, has word lists for first grade through sixth grade. Each word list also has sentences for dictation. The teacher would dictate, or say a sentence aloud. Students had to write all of the words in the sentence just as the teacher said them. They had to spell all of the words correctly. Students also studied their spelling words by writing them in poems and rhymes. This spelling textbook has a message to students: "For a few pupils spelling may never be easy, but it is something most of us use all the time, and, as a rule, we think those who cannot spell common words do not know much."

Some teachers made spelling fun with spelling bees, or "spell downs." Everyone lined up at the front of the room. The teacher said a word to spell aloud. The student repeated the word, then spelled the word, then said the word again. For example, "Blackboard, b-l-a-c-k-b-o-a-r-d, blackboard." If you did not spell the word correctly, you were out of the competition. Depending on the age of each speller, the next student might have to spell the misspelled word in order to stay in the bee. The last student to spell a word correctly became the winner.

**GRADE THREE—PART TWO**

FIRST WEEK

Review of the Hardest Words Already Studied

Success in any study depends upon your mastering each step day by day. Otherwise troubles grow daily.

| | | | | |
|---|---|---|---|---|
| across | dear | just | read | two |
| again | die | know | ready | until |
| always | does | laid | right | used |
| any | done | led | road | very |
| apple | early | many | rode | wait |
| asked | easy | much | rule | warm |
| aunt | eight | near | running | wear |
| babies | eleven | noise | said | week |
| been | every | noisy | school | were |
| before | fair | none | second | what |
| blue | forty | off | sent | when |
| brave | fruit | once | shoes | where |
| bread | goes | one | shows | white |
| buy | hear | only | some | who |
| can't | here | own | stick | whole |
| cents | high | plate | such | why |
| city | house | please | sure | wife |
| clean | ice | pocket | they | write |
| color | its | pure | too | yellow |

13

Grade-three students used this list of spelling words. Do you think "troubles grow daily" if you don't work hard in school? *The New National Speller,* 1926

The Friday spell-down will begin at 1:00 P.M. All grades!

A spell down was also called a spelling bee. Photo by Susan Apps-Bodilly

Jerry remembers practicing spelling at home with his mother and brothers. He says, "We had special radio programs we listened to: *The Lone Ranger*, *Terry and the Pirates*, and *Captain Midnight*. We couldn't listen to our programs until our work was done. Every night we had a school session with our mother which always included spelling." Listening to the radio was very fun and entertaining for the whole family in the evening after chores were finished—television was not widely available in 1939.

In most one-room schools, arithmetic was just as important as learning to read. The teacher wrote math problems for each grade in

addition, subtraction, multiplication, and division on the chalkboard
for students to copy and solve. The teacher organized students into
groups based on their ability. A third-grade student could be in a
group with fourth- and fifth-grade students. Each group came to
the front of the room to meet with the teacher, as they did with
reading groups. The teacher could check their work and students
could ask questions. Often, the teacher would try to connect math
story problems to situations on the farm. In this way, students
knew that working with numbers related to their daily life at home.
Students also learned about counting money, the calendar, measuring,
fractions, and telling time.

The youngest students in the one-room schoolhouse learned to
print the letters of the alphabet. However, learning to read and write
in cursive was more important. All of the letters connect in cursive,
making it a faster way of writing. At the front of each classroom
above the blackboard was an alphabet strip with the small and capital
letters of the Palmer Method. This method, developed by Austin
Palmer in 1894, became the most popular handwriting system in the
United States. Students made many circles and ovals as practice for
making each letter. Often students who were naturally left handed
were taught to write with their other hand. A student who wrote
with his or her left hand was thought to be not writing "correctly."
The Writing grade on the Chain O' Lake report card was for
handwriting. Today, a grade for writing usually means writing stories
or research reports. Teachers in the one-room school usually had
beautiful, flowing cursive writing. Students were expected to try their
best to do the same.

The teacher wrote reading and penmanship lessons on the chalkboard. You can see old readers at the Rhinelander School Museum. **Photo by Susan Apps-Bodilly**

Country school students were familiar with many aspects of science as part of their daily lives. They saw mother cows giving birth to calves, raised chickens, grew potatoes and strawberries, and spent time outside enjoying nature. They observed the changing seasons on their walks to school, listened to birds, and collected and identified different kinds of rocks, such as quartz and granite, at recess. As part of a farm family, they were well aware of how the weather, such as rain, hail, and drought, **influenced** how well the corn and hay crops grew every summer.

**influenced** (**in** floo uhnsd): affected someone or something

Science was part of the school day as well. Many graduates of one-room schools remember studying science as a chance to experience nature first hand. If the school was near a pond or a neighbor's woods, students could walk and observe the plants and animals living there. In the fall, they collected and identified leaves and made collections. In the winter, they studied hibernation, snowfall, and bird and animal tracks. In the spring, there were wildflowers, new plants, budding trees, insects, and rainstorms.

The Chain O' Lake schoolhouse had an open wooden box that stood on 4 legs. There was sand in the box. Using this box, Miss Piechowski could demonstrate all sorts of science lessons. She could show the effects of soil erosion by building a hill of sand and pouring water in the box to show how the "soil" would run down the hill. Then, she could demonstrate how to avoid soil erosion by "planting" twigs and leaves, which were meant to be trees, to stop the soil runoff. The one-room schoolhouse at the Pioneer Park Historical Complex in Rhinelander has a science box filled with sand. Today, visitors can use the box to practice science as students of the past did.

Top: Ruth Olson grew up on this dairy farm in Vernon County. She and other students in the country learned a lot about science topics from living on a farm. **Courtesy of Ruth Olson Apps**
Bottom: This sand tray is on display at the Pioneer Park Historical Complex in Rhinelander. Teachers used this tray for science lessons. **Photo by Susan Apps-Bodilly**

Maps, like this one at the Rhinelander School Museum, help students learn about places around the world. Do you have maps in your classroom today? Photo by Susan Apps-Bodilly

Many students in schools in Wisconsin had parents or grandparents who **emigrated** from other countries to the United States. An important part of going to school was learning to speak, read, and write in English. Many families spoke another language, such as German or Swedish, at home. Most parents wanted their children to learn English, so they could become more "American."

Participating in school in the United States of America also meant learning about important places and people in United States history. For example, students learned about Thomas Jefferson, the third

**emigrated** (**em** uh gray tid): left one's own country to settle in another

president. He believed that a free public education was a way to build a strong democratic country. They also learned about the sixteenth president, Abraham Lincoln.

With maps and globes in the classroom, students learned about places around the world. Students also used the *Weekly Reader* to find out about current events. In 1939, Jerry learned that Germany and England were already at war with each other. He remembers reading about the conflict between the countries in Europe when he was in school. In the coming years, the United States would join this war—World War II. By studying subjects such as civics, geography, and history, the Chain O' Lake students learned how to be good citizens.

Darrel, Jerry, and Donald Apps are pictured near the back porch of their farmhouse on the first day of school. They each carried their own lunch bucket. **Courtesy of Jerry Apps**

# Chapter 8

# Lunch Hour

Just like you, children in the one-room school looked forward to a break from their lessons. Lunchtime began at noon and lasted for one hour. One-room schools did not have a cafeteria or lunchroom. Students ate outside, either on the school steps or under a tree in the schoolyard. On rainy days, they stayed inside and ate at their desks. To keep warm on **blustery** winter days, students sometimes ate lunch near the woodstove.

In the morning, mothers prepared lunch with foods from the family farm; fathers were usually already out

---

**blustery** (**bluhs** tur ee): having stormy weather with strong wind

European American and African American farm families of Pleasant Ridge built this school in 1870 for all of the children in the community. It was located in Beetown Township in Grant County. It is believed to be one of the earliest schools in Wisconsin to integrate, or to allow all races to attend the school. Did you notice the student with his lunch pail? **WHi Image ID 4239**

in the barn. Children carried food in a lunch bucket. The bucket was made from an empty **lard** pail or a Karo syrup pail. It had a lid and a metal handle for carrying it to school. In 1939, no one had fancy lunch boxes or even paper bags to carry their lunches.

What did students eat for lunch? A typical lunch was a bologna or peanut butter and jelly sandwich on homemade bread or biscuits. The sandwiches were sometimes wrapped in wax paper. In 1939, plastic wrap and aluminum foil were not yet available. During harvest season, there was a fresh piece of fruit, such as an apple. Special

**lard** (lahrd): white grease used for cooking, made from melted fat

lunch treats might be a cookie or cake, a hard-boiled egg, or a pickle. Children from the poorest families sometimes did not bring a lunch or perhaps had only a slice of bread. Other children happily shared their food with them.

Children brought a **pint jar** of milk to drink. This milk was not **pasteurized**—it was milk straight from the dairy cows milked that morning. Jerry did not like the taste of warm milk. In the winter, he found a way to make the milk taste better, and he told his friends. Before school, his mother mixed chocolate syrup in with the milk. At morning recess, he stuck his jar of milk outside in the snow! Can you picture all of the jars of milk cooling in the snow next to the schoolhouse steps? At lunchtime, he and his classmates drank delicious jars of cold chocolate milk. Can you think like a historian and guess why cold milk was a special treat?

During the long Wisconsin winters, a pan of water always sat on the woodstove. Heat from a stove made the schoolroom air dry. The water in the pan would heat up, **evaporate**, and put moisture in the

This display at the Halfway Prairie School shows the different ways students used to bring their lunch to school. Can you tell which are older? Which ones are newer? Photo by Susan Apps-Bodilly

**pint jar** (**pɪnt jahr**): a jar that can hold 16 fluid ounces

**pasteurized** (**pas** chuh rɪzd): the state of milk after it has been heated to a high temperature to kill harmful bacteria

**evaporate** (i **vap** uh rayt): change into vapor and become part of the air

This young girl prepares a school lunch on a stove. WHi Image ID 43904

air. This pan of water also cooked lunch! In addition to milk, Jerry and his classmates brought food in pint jars. The jars contained chili, tomato or potato soup, or baked beans with hot dogs or sauerkraut. The warm water heated up the food in each jar. After morning recess, students put their lunch jars into the pan of water and loosened the metal ring and lid. After the students set the jars in the water, the teacher checked each one carefully. A jar with a tight lid would heat up too much, expand, and explode. Jerry was always hoping one would explode—that would certainly bring some excitement to a cold winter day! Not one ever did.

Lily Wolff remembers "Soup Fridays" during the winter in her one-room school. On those days, each student would bring something to add to a big pot of soup. One student brought "drippings," which were the fat and juices from cooked meat. Others brought carrots, onions, barley, meat, and potatoes. Imagine the wonderful smell of soup in the classroom all morning while you worked on reading and arithmetic. Lunchtime could not come soon enough!

Sometimes friends traded their lunch food. Ruth Olson remembers when her friend Charlotte brought store-bought cookies in her lunch. She felt jealous! The marshmallow filling and chocolate looked delicious. Ruth's mother did not spend money on cookies from the store because they made cookies at home. Ruth traded one of her homemade molasses cookies for one of Charlotte's store-bought ones. Friends eating in the schoolyard enjoyed lunch together just as you do today.

# Think about the Past

These pages are from a recipe booklet published in 1923 by the Educational Department, Royal Baking Powder Company, New York. What can you learn about children's lunches in the past from this primary source? Do you see anything that you would like to eat for lunch?

The recipe book included these instructions for mothers about packing a school lunch:

*The daintiest lunch in the world can be spoiled in packing. Cut sandwiches thin and into "lady fingers" or attractive pieces, easy to eat, and wrap each individually in wax paper. A covered jelly glass or screw top jar nicely holds a baked apple. A custard or chocolate pudding can be packed in the cup in which it was baked, and don't forget the spoon.*

*Remember, too, that boys hate to fuss with desserts if compelled to carry a cup or spoon home; an apple or other raw fruit is better for the boy's lunch box.*

*Do not skimp the eggs, whole milk or butter when preparing recipes for children and try to use more often the whole wheat and coarser flours rather than the regulation plain wheat flour.*

Did you notice the suggestion to use a jelly glass jar and wax paper? What do you think it means that some boys of the past didn't want to carry home a spoon? Did you notice the instructions didn't say this about girls? Why did mothers view boys and girls differently in the past?

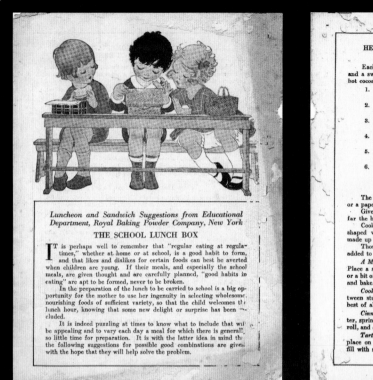

*Luncheon and Sandwich Suggestions from Educational Department, Royal Baking Powder Company, New York*

### THE SCHOOL LUNCH BOX

IT is perhaps well to remember that "regular eating at regular times," whether at home or at school, is a good habit to form, and that likes and dislikes for certain foods can best be averted when children are young. If their meals, and especially the school meals, are given thought and are carefully planned, "good habits in eating" are apt to be formed, never to be broken.

In the preparation of the lunch to be carried to school is a big opportunity for the mother to use her ingenuity in selecting wholesome, nourishing foods of sufficient variety, so that the child welcomes the lunch hour, knowing that some new delight or surprise has been included.

It is indeed puzzling at times to know what to include that will be appealing and to vary each day a meal for which there is generally so little time for preparation. It is with the latter idea in mind that the following suggestions for possible good combinations are given with the hope that they will help solve the problem.

### HEARTY BUT WHOLESOME COMBINATIONS FOR THE SCHOOL LUNCH BOX

Each lunch should include a meaty sandwich, a refreshing drink, and a sweet; any of the following with a glass of milk or a cup of hot cocoa makes a light but adequate lunch:

1. Date bread sandwiches spread with butter or cream cheese, peanut cookies, orange.
2. Biscuit sandwiches with chopped chicken, banana, two or three pieces of fudge.
3. Biscuit sandwiches with crisp lettuce, cup custard, filled cookies.
4. Graham biscuit sandwiches with chopped meat filling, home-made Cinnamon Buns, stewed apricots in custard cup.
5. Brown bread and butter sandwich, custard cup of baked beans, whole tomato, Raisin Drop Cakes.
6. Whole wheat fruit bread sandwiches, cheese and pineapple filling, Chocolate Cup Cake with Icing.

#### Things That Children Love To See

The unexpected always pleases children and a new cookie, muffin, or a paper of candies, included in the lunch, will delight them.

Give them foods that will require chewing: coarse flours are by far the best to use in breads, muffins and cookies.

Cookies made with fancy cutters—animal shapes, stars, etc., or shaped with ordinary knife or Royal can cover (crescents); also made up with jam or icing additions.

Those not fond of carrots will like them finely shredded and added to mayonnaise or served with a lemon parsley sauce.

*A Muffin Surprise*—Put a tablespoon of muffin batter into a tin. Place a stoned date, a piece of pineapple, a teaspoon chopped ham, or a bit of red jelly in center. Cover with another tablespoon of batter and bake.

*Cookie Delights*—Place one cookie atop another with an in-between stuffing of marshmallow, ground raisins, nut butter, jam, or, best of all, ground figs.

*Cinnamon Buns*—Spread the thinly rolled biscuit dough with butter, sprinkle with cinnamon and plenty of brown sugar, roll like jelly roll, and cut in one and one-half inch slices and bake.

*Tart*—Roll biscuit dough thin, cut hole in center of one biscuit, place on top of another buttered biscuit, press together; bake and fill with stewed cranberries or other fruit or jam.

This booklet about school lunches was printed by the Royal Baking Powder Company in 1923. Do you agree that lunch should include a "sandwich, a refreshing drink, and a sweet"? **"The School Lunch Box," 1923**

Schoolchildren in Madison listening to a Philco radio at the front of their classroom, 1931. **WHi Image ID 18402**

# Chapter 9

## Music, Nature Study, Art, and the Radio

Every school day began outside with the raising of the flag and the Pledge of Allegiance. The flag was always up on the flagpole if school was in session. After the flag ceremony, the teacher and students filed inside. Many one-room schools had a piano at the front of the room. On cold days, the teacher played a marching tune and students stomped around the room until they warmed up!

A popular music book in country schools was *The Golden Book of Favorite Songs*. It has **patriotic** songs such as "America the Beautiful" and "Yankee Doodle." There are also

**patriotic** (pay tree **ot** ik): showing love and loyalty for one's country

# Patriotism in the Classroom

Inside the front cover of *The Golden Book of Favorite Songs* is a quote from the Declaration of Independence. The children recited it in unison:

*We hold these truths to be self-evident:*
*That all men are created equal;*
*That they are endowed by their Creator with certain inalienable rights;*
*That among these are life, liberty, and the pursuit of happiness;*
*That to secure these rights, governments are instituted among men, deriving their just powers from the consent of the governed.*

This quote is an example of patriotism, or an expression of love for the country where one lives. Patriotism and learning to be a good citizen were important in the one-room schools.

songs that are fun to sing in a "round," such as "Row, Row, Row Your Boat" and "Are You Sleeping?" A round is a special song to sing. The students are divided into 2 groups. Each group sings the same melody, but each group begins at a different time. Their singing fits together in harmony. A round sounds beautiful. Some songs for the youngest children were the nursery rhymes, such as "Baa! Baa! Black Sheep" and "Hey, Diddle Diddle."

Many one-room schools did not have electricity. Listening to the Philco battery-operated radio was a popular part of many school days. The University of Wisconsin started broadcasting educational radio programs in the 1920s. Known as the *Wisconsin School of the*

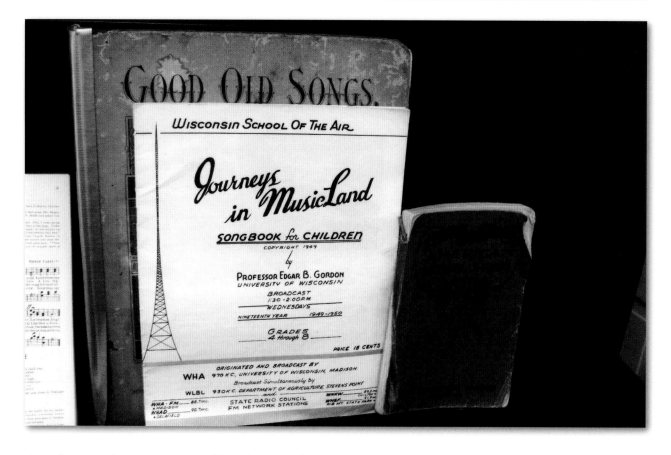

*Air*, these radio programs offered a way for students all over the state to listen and learn from university professors.

A favorite show was "Journeys in Music Land." Edgar B. Gordon, or "Pop Gordon," a music professor from the university, presented this program. Students had a copy of the songbook for the show. They learned to sing and read music notes. They listened to Pop Gordon tell the history of each song. Then, he gave a demonstration of how to sing it. The show had a theme song that everyone knew: "Sing, sing the whole day through. The best of things will come to you. A song will always see you through, so sing, just sing." In the spring, a highlight for some students was a visit to Madison for a gathering of

On Wednesday afternoons from 1:30 to 2:00, students tuned in to hear Professor Gordon from the University of Wisconsin on the radio. He taught music to children all over the state with his radio show called "Journeys in Music Land." These music books sit on the piano at the Halfway Prairie School. Photo by Susan Apps-Bodilly

Students who listened to Professor Gordon's program during the year traveled to the University of Wisconsin in the spring to sing with him. Here he is conducting a piece of music at the 1950 gathering in the Stock Pavilion on the Madison campus. **WHi Image ID 65313**

the program's listeners. Many students came to join Pop Gordon for a broadcast at the Stock Pavilion on campus. Together, they could sing all of the songs they learned from him during the year.

One of Jerry's favorite *Wisconsin School of the Air* shows on Monday mornings was "Afield with Ranger Mac." This program was about nature. He remembers the deep voice of Wakelin McNeel, who presented this radio program from 1933 to 1954. Mr. McNeel was also a professor at the University of Wisconsin. The program was only 15 minutes long, but it provided interesting information about science and nature. Nicknamed "Ranger Mac," McNeel promoted the idea of having a "school forest" to study. He encouraged schoolchildren to plant trees as an educational project to help them learn to care for a forest habitat. He also suggested that students have a nature corner in the classroom and keep a log of nature happenings. The program's teacher's guide included extra activities that students could do and things they could try at home. Each program ended with, "May the Great Spirit put sunshine in your hearts, now and forever more. Heap much!" (When Ranger Mac said *heap much*, he meant *gain much*.)

Another popular program on *Wisconsin School of the Air* was "Let's Draw." Jim Schwalbach was the University of Wisconsin

# A Game of Musical Chairs

Some one-room schools had a wind-up record player and a few records of marching band music. A fun music game to play was musical chairs. Do you know how to play this game? To play, line up chairs in a circle or in 2 rows. There must be one chair less than the number of people, so if there are 10 children, start with 9 chairs. Everyone marches around the chairs in time to the music. When the music stops, sit down quickly in a chair! The person who does not find a chair to sit in is out. Take one chair away each time. The game continues until there are only 2 students left and one chair. The person who sits in the last chair is the winner.

For 21 years, Wakelin McNeel taught a nature program called "Afield with Ranger Mac." The program was heard on the radio. **Courtesy of the UW Archives, Image #S05827**

professor who taught this class. Students listened to his voice as he used music, stories, poetry, or a drama to give them ideas for pictures. They used crayons or pencils to make drawings. They also used wet paper with paints for watercolor paintings. The radio art teacher encouraged the children to be creative and let the colors run together. For many students, this was their first introduction to the idea of being artistic with color.

By the end of the 1930s, there were many *Wisconsin School of the Air* programs offered on the radio to students and their teachers. Programs about geography, French, history, and theater were important additions to the school day. The battery-operated radio was a way to connect schools across the state that could get the radio signal. It tied them all together. There could be 50,000 Wisconsin children listening at the same time. Using the radio for education became part of the **Wisconsin Idea**. This meant that the University of Wisconsin was available to anyone and everyone, all over the state. The University of Wisconsin President Charles Van Hise and Governor Robert La Follette planned a way to connect the research and information from the university to Wisconsin citizens. They wanted to help people learn new things that could enrich their lives. A person listening to the radio could learn things from professors at the university without even traveling to Madison.

By 1931, the *Wisconsin School of the Air* over the WHA radio station was offering school programs in civics, music, art, nature study, and health. There were also programs for adults. One popular

**Wisconsin Idea** (wi-**skon**-suhn ɪ-**dee**-uh): the goal that knowledge and developments from the University of Wisconsin will be used to benefit those living in the state

program taught about nutrition, clothing, and cooking for mothers working at home.

Jerry remembers looking forward to the time of day when the teacher turned on the radio. He and his classmates stopped whatever lesson they were doing when it was time for a program to start. Each program was on once a week. Miss Piechowski was very clear about the rules for the school radio. They did not listen to the radio unless an educational program was on. A child who turned on the radio when there was no program was in big trouble because the battery was expensive. Nobody wanted the battery to run out. They would miss their programs.

Students, from tallest to shortest, spell out the word *Christmas* during a program in December 1946 at James Otis School in Fond du Lac County. **Courtesy of Mary Hanley**

# Chapter 10

## The Christmas Program

The biggest celebration and the social event of the school year was the annual Christmas program. Lily Wolff, the teacher from Wildwood School in northern Wisconsin, remembers that she began planning for this program well before the weather turned cold. Miss Wolff recalls, "If you could put on an excellent Christmas program, you were an excellent teacher. Some of my teacher friends even spent their own money to be sure it would be good." The entire community looked forward to this gathering. All families were invited. Neighbors who did not have school-age children also came. The show was held in the evening, just before the school's winter break.

Each program at the Chain O' Lake School had a theme: the songs and poems were about snow, snowmen, winter, cold weather, or Santa. Some schools did an entire Christmas manger scene with Mary, Joseph, and the baby Jesus.

On the Monday after Thanksgiving, students at the Chain O' Lake School began preparing for the program. They continued all of their regular classes, but every day in the afternoon children began learning songs and poems to recite. Everyone participated, from the youngest first graders to the oldest eighth graders. These weeks of preparation incorporated many kinds of learning: reciting a poem with good expression, singing, building and setting up a stage with curtains, making costumes, and planning the order of the show. The older students helped the younger ones learn their lines. While the older students practiced, the younger ones made paper chains and tissue-paper snowflakes. It took the best efforts and cooperation of everyone to put on a great show.

A typical program had 2 or 3 small skits put on by groups of children. The teacher chose the parts for each student based on what he or she could do. In between the skits, there was a performance by a singing **quartet** or a special **solo**. The teacher or a parent accompanied the singers on the piano.

Each student also recited a poem. The program ended with a grand **finale** group song, which included everyone in the school.

The weekend before the big performance at the Chain O' Lake School, the fathers on the school board pulled down long wooden

**quartet** (kwor **tet**): a group of 4 people playing music or singing together

**solo** (**soh** loh): part of a song performed by one person

**finale** (fuh **nal** ee): the last part of a performance or show

These girls perform a song for a holiday program. Do you see the fabric hanging on a wire? This is the curtain for the "stage."
**Courtesy of Mary Hanley**

boards from their storage place in the woodshed. Mr. Swendryznski, Mildred's father, dragged the boards into the schoolhouse and put them on top of **sawhorses**. Mr. Jenks, the neighbor who helped build the fire in the morning, nailed the boards to the sawhorses to hold them in place. The stage was made of boards nailed to sawhorses that were about 2 feet high. The stage was high enough that everyone could see the performers on the stage. Parents strung a wire across the front of the room. On this wire, they attached some bedsheets, which became a curtain for the stage. At each side, more bedsheets

**sawhorse** (**saw** hors): a stand used to support pieces of wood that are being sawed

on wires formed 2 "dressing rooms": one for the boys and one for the girls. The stage was ready! During the last week of rehearsal, the students could practice on a real stage. To get up on the stage, students stepped up from a chair. They had 5 more days to prepare.

When he was in first grade, Jerry was assigned the opening line of the Christmas show. He had been in school for only 4 months. He was sure he would not be able to speak in front of the huge crowd by himself. His teacher Miss Piechowski told him, "Do not look at the faces in the audience. Just look out past them to the stovepipe in the back of the room."

On the night of the program, Jerry remembers that he wore new overalls, a new flannel shirt, and shiny shoes. The room was filled from one end to the other with people, including his family and the entire neighborhood. The 2 gas lanterns hanging from the ceiling cast interesting shadows below. The stove was burning and the room was very warm because of all the people. When the time came to begin the Christmas program, Jerry stood up on the stage in front of everyone, took a big breath, and said, "We welcome you to our program!" His voice was brave and loud for everyone to hear. He did not notice the big smiles on the faces of his parents and the silly, teasing faces of his little brothers because he was looking at the back of the room toward the stovepipe. Miss Piechowski's advice had worked!

At Ruth Olson's school in Vernon County, students **exchanged** names to receive and give gifts. They exchanged gifts right after the Christmas program, while the families were all there. "Everyone chose a slip of paper with the name of another student on it. Then,

---

**exchanged** (eks **chaynjd**): gave one thing for another

you brought a gift for that person and put it under the Christmas tree," Ruth remembers. "I was so excited to give a gift to my friend Charlotte's older brother. It was a Roy Rogers cowboy book. Roy Rogers was a cowboy character that everyone loved from the radio. I thought her brother was wonderful because he was older than me."

Many school programs ended with a special holiday visitor. Ruth remembers the excitement of hearing the jingle of sleigh bells outside of the school building. Everyone inside knew this meant that Santa had arrived! "Santa Claus would come into the crowded room with a loud, 'Ho, ho, ho! Merry Christmas!' Sometimes he brought a bag of peanuts in the shell, candy canes, or some hard Christmas candy," she says.

Santa also visited the Christmas program at Jerry's school. One year, Santa burst through the door with a loud "Ho, ho, ho!" that woke up the babies and made them cry. He stomped the snow off his boots, ran up to the front of the room, and kissed the teacher on the cheek. Jerry says, "The teacher's face turned a bright red, everyone laughed and it was just great fun." Christmas gifts were usually very practical. They were things the children needed for school, not toys. Santa had a new pencil or a notebook for everyone.

Joe Sveda went to a one-room school called Badger School, which was north of Antigo. When he started school at age 6, he did not speak English. At home, his family only spoke Czechoslovakian. Joe remembers, "I don't recall how much English I understood, but I seemed to get along with the teacher real well. My teacher did not understand my language, but she seemed to know if I understood what she was saying in English by my facial expressions. If I looked puzzled when I talked, then she would know I did not understand. Some Polish families were our closest neighbors; I could understand

# Family Traditions

Not all families in one-room schools were Christians who celebrated Christmas. In fact, families in one-room schools were often from many cultures. They may have celebrated holidays in different ways at home.

Here are some of the families from Jerry's school and their **ethnic group**:

- Apps: English and German
- Davies: Welsh
- Hudziak: Polish

- Kolka: Czechoslovakian
- Korleski: Polish
- Miller: German
- Nelson: Norwegian

- Swendryznski: Polish
- York: English

Each family had their own holiday traditions of food, decorations, and songs that were part of their family history. Jerry's family always ate oyster stew on Christmas Eve. They enjoyed many German meat products, such as head cheese. (Head cheese is not cheese, but a meat jelly made from the head of a calf or pig.) They also ate lots of sauerkraut, or sour cabbage. The Polish families also ate sauerkraut, but many of the Norwegians, Welsh, and English families did not like it! What holiday traditions do your friends have? Do you learn about other cultures at school today?

---

**ethnic group** (eth **nik**  group): a group of people sharing the same home country or culture

a few things they said in Polish, but not a lot. They could also speak English. So, I was the only one learning English when I got to school."

In December, the county superintendent told Joe's teacher that he would have to learn English by the end of the year in order to pass to the next grade. Joe's teacher did not agree with this rule. However, she found a way to help Joe learn to speak in English. She kept him after school. She told him she needed extra help. While the teacher and Joe put things up on the bulletin boards, she told him to repeat rhyming phrases over and over in English. Joe remembers, "After 2 weeks, I came to school and repeated 'Little Boy Blue' for her—the whole thing! She was so happy."

Joe remembers how he worked to pass second grade. "It took me 2 weeks to learn that first rhyme. Once I did, I started talking and my teacher could not shut me up! I remember it as if it was today," he says. "That woman was such a motivating person. How did she have time to care? I am sure she cared for every kid like that. She was strict, but she was just a marvel." When the time came for the Christmas program, Joe participated with everyone else.

The one-room school annual Christmas program was a special event that joined neighbors who may have spoken different languages and had different holiday traditions. The families were alike because all the parents wanted to support the teacher. Even neighbors who did not have children came to the program because they knew the importance of a good education for the children in the community. Jerry remembers a special neighbor coming to his Christmas programs. John Forsythe was a bachelor who lived near the school. He was not married and did not have any children who attended the school. However, he came to the school's program each year. He was so fond of seeing the children perform that he brought a treat for them: Red Delicious apples. In winter, fresh fruit was expensive, so this was a special gift for each child in the school.

# Learning to Speak English

Joe Sveda's family did not speak English at home. They spoke Czechoslovakian. Nursery rhymes helped Joe learn to speak in English. Here are the words to "Little Boy Blue," the first rhyme Joe memorized:

Little Boy Blue,
Come blow your horn,
The sheep's in the meadow,
The cow's in the corn;

Where is that boy
Who looks after the sheep?
Under the haystack
Fast asleep.

Will you wake him?
Oh no, not I,
For if I do
He will surely cry.

There was an unspoken understanding among everyone that supporting the school was important. The standing-room-only group that filled the one-room school on the night of the Christmas program showed the entire neighborhood coming together in support of their school and the children of their community.

Above: Teachers gave each student a Christmas card or a souvenir booklet as a holiday gift. Herman Apps, Jerry's father, got this postcard from his teacher when he was in fifth grade. Miss Simon is pictured on the front. Later, she married Herman's older brother John. Herman's teacher became his sister-in-law! Left: This souvenir Christmas booklet was given to Jerry's mother, Eleanora Witt in 1916. She began school in a one-room schoolhouse in Kellner, Wisconsin. In this school, everyone spoke German. Later, the family moved and Elenora attended the Chain O' Lake School. Her teacher Miss Murty is pictured on the front. Inside is a list of the 22 students, including Elenora's younger brothers Harry and Wilbur. **Collection of Susan Apps-Bodilly**

Students at Riverview School in Dunn County in 1937. Do you see their lunch pails? They are roasting food on sticks over a fire. Students often had a special celebration like this after cleaning up the schoolyard on Arbor Day. **Courtesy of Janet Creaser**

Students in one-room schools worked hard on their lessons. However, there was also time for celebrations. Members of the school board and the students' mothers often helped with food and activities at school. There were special days during all parts of the school year for fun. Do you enjoy parties at school?

In the fall, most schools held a Halloween party. At the Chain O' Lake School, Jerry's teacher set up a way to "frighten" someone at the Halloween party. A brave volunteer put on a blindfold. While he touched the items without looking, the teacher told everyone a spooky story. She described the "eyeballs" and "brain" that were on the table. The eyeballs were really pieces of fruit and the brain was a bowl of noodles! It was fun to feel scared and pretend.

The month of November brought 2 celebration times. Jerry remembers a special day on November 11: Armistice Day. At the eleventh hour (11:00 a.m.) of the eleventh day of the eleventh month of the year, all of the students in the school stood up with respect and faced east. They were turning toward the direction of Europe, where the **armistice** was signed in 1918 between the Allies of World War I and Germany to call a **cease-fire**. This day was not a party day, but a special day of celebration of the peace between countries. Today, we continue to celebrate Veterans Day on November 11 to honor all men and women who have served, or are now serving, our country.

During the week before Thanksgiving, students made paper cutouts of turkeys from construction paper. They learned about the pilgrims who traveled to the United States from Europe. The teacher talked with students about the Indians who helped the pilgrims survive by planting fish with their corn seeds. There was no school on Thanksgiving and the next day.

Most schools had pictures of George Washington and Abraham Lincoln displayed at the front of the room. On February 12, students made black construction paper **silhouettes** of Lincoln. On the third Monday of February, students celebrated Washington's birthday. They learned that he was the first president and the "Father of Our Country."

---

**armistice** (**ahr** muh stis): an agreement between enemy countries to stop a war

**cease-fire** (**sees fɪr**): the end of the fighting of a war

**silhouette** (sil oo **et**): a dark outline visible against a light background]

On February 14, Valentine's Day, teachers invited families to come to the Valentine's Day party. Mothers brought cookies or cake to share.

Ruth Olson Apps remembers a big box in front of the room. "The box had frilly, tissue-paper hearts decorating each side. Each student brought a valentine for everyone else, including the teacher," she says. "During the week, we brought our valentines and put them all in the big box. On Valentine's Day, during the party, the valentines were delivered. Most valentines were all handmade." The cards often had special sayings of affection on them, like "Be mine" and "Who loves you? I do!" Ruth made a valentine in the shape of a small chalkboard. Her clever valentine said, "You can't rub out my love for you." If you did not want a person to know that you gave him or her a valentine, you signed it "Secret Admirer."

In February, students celebrated the birthdays of George Washington and Abraham Lincoln. Their pictures were on the wall of most one-room schools. WHi Image ID 41020

Ruth Olson made this valentine in school to give to her mother. She tied a piece of tissue to the paper with string. It is made to look like a small chalkboard. Do you make valentines at school for your friends and family? Courtesy of Ruth Olson Apps

The spring season was particularly welcome at the one-room schoolhouse. After a long, cold winter, the children could have a celebration outside. Marilyn Hanson Apps remembers spring at the Pine River School. She explains that on Arbor Day in April everyone brought a rake to school. At many one-room schools, the teacher and students were expected to "observe" this day by "beautifying the school grounds." It was likely a welcome change to be outside, even to clean up the entire schoolyard. "Everyone spent time raking leaves and dead grass into a big pile. We had a good-sized schoolyard, so this took a while," she recalls. "When we were done, we could look for sticks by the river. We piled up the sticks on the dead leaves and the teacher started a fire. Everyone brought hot dogs and marshmallows from home and roasted them over the fire." At some schools, an important part of Arbor Day was the planting of a new tree in the schoolyard. Students helped take care of their own schoolyard with these Arbor Day traditions.

On May 1, many children celebrated spring with May baskets. At school, they wove strips of construction paper into baskets and pasted on a handle. They picked spring flowers to put in each basket. On that night, Jerry and his little brothers went out to deliver them. "We would walk from farm to farm and hang a basket on the door and yell, 'May basket!' Then, we ran away and hid. The kids inside had to catch you, and if they did, they would join up and go along to the next place," he recalls. "The farms were far apart—we walked miles across farm fields just to deliver a few baskets. It was fun, but a little exciting, too: a dog might chase you or you ripped your pants climbing over a wire fence."

At the end of the year, the eighth-grade students had to pass an important county examination before they could go on to the high school in town for ninth grade. The eighth-grade students worked all year for this test. They studied in school and at home. It took many hours of extra work. On the big day of the test, eighth graders from all of the one-room schools across the county gathered in town to take this daylong test. Students were tested on reading, penmanship, spelling, grammar, arithmetic, geography, United States history, civics, and science. The test results came in the mail 2 weeks later. Students who passed this test received an eighth-grade diploma from the school superintendent at the county courthouse during a graduation ceremony. It was an honor and a great accomplishment to pass this test and complete 8 years of school.

As it is today, the last day of school was a favorite day for the students and the teacher. At the one-room schoolhouse, the last day was another day for the entire community to come together. At the Chain O' Lake School, the main feature of this day was the noon potluck lunch. The same boards that had been a stage in December were carried outside. Fathers set them up on the sawhorses as makeshift tables. Each family brought their own dishes, silverware, sandwiches, and a "dish to pass," which was food to be shared. Many graduates of one-room schools remember this day as "the one with

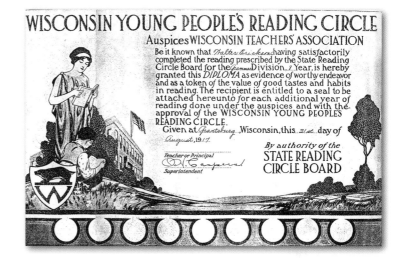

This is an example of a reading award for year 8.
**Courtesy of Jerry Apps**

Parents and children looked forward to special celebrations at school. Everyone is eating and talking at this party in the Chain O' Lake School in the late 1940s. **Courtesy of Jerry Apps**

a lot of food." The teacher brought ice cream packed in insulated containers so it would not melt. The school board paid for the ice cream as an end-of-the-year treat.

A fun tradition on the last day was the annual fathers **versus** children softball game. For many, this was the only time of the year that they saw their fathers play. Most farm men were very busy all year with work on their farms. Jerry remembers that his student softball team was usually pretty good by the end of the year, after

**versus** (**vur** suhs): against

Children and their families gather for a game of softball in the spring of 1951 at South Bright School in Clark County. **Courtesy of Esther Luke Niedzwiecki**

practicing during recess all spring. "The fathers had not played since last year's picnic. It was always fun to watch the fathers try to hit the ball. Some would take a mighty swing, miss the ball, and fall down! Some would hit the ball and it would fly out of the schoolyard and into the neighbor's field," he remembers. "The teacher would organize all of the games, like a 3-legged race for the younger children who didn't want to play softball. The mothers would enjoy talking under the shade of the pine trees."

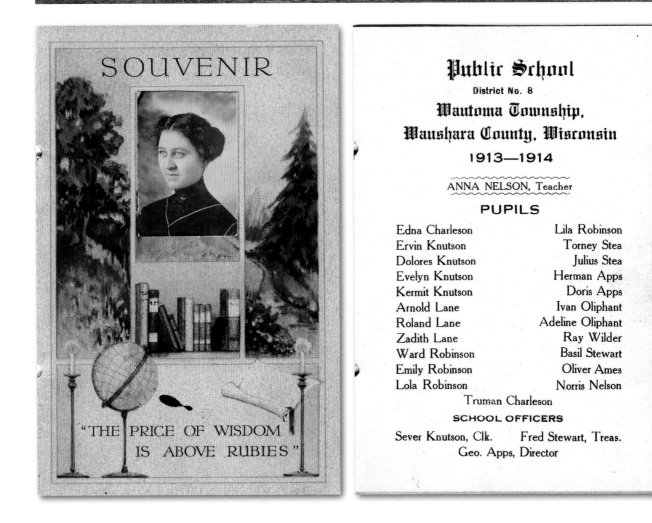

SOUVENIR

"THE PRICE OF WISDOM
IS ABOVE RUBIES"

**Public School**
District No. 8
**Wautoma Township,
Waushara County, Wisconsin**
1913—1914

ANNA NELSON, Teacher

**PUPILS**

| | |
|---|---|
| Edna Charleson | Lila Robinson |
| Ervin Knutson | Torney Stea |
| Dolores Knutson | Julius Stea |
| Evelyn Knutson | Herman Apps |
| Kermit Knutson | Doris Apps |
| Arnold Lane | Ivan Oliphant |
| Roland Lane | Adeline Oliphant |
| Zadith Lane | Ray Wilder |
| Ward Robinson | Basil Stewart |
| Emily Robinson | Oliver Ames |
| Lola Robinson | Norris Nelson |

Truman Charleson

**SCHOOL OFFICERS**

Sever Knutson, Clk.      Fred Stewart, Treas.
Geo. Apps, Director

At left is the cover of a souvenir booklet that Herman Apps received from his teacher as a gift in 1914. The teacher, Anna Nelson, is pictured on the front. Inside is a list of all of the students, the teacher, and the school officers. Do you know why many students have the same last name? **Courtesy of Jerry Apps**

As the picnic ended, everyone said good-bye to the teacher for the summer, sometimes with a little end-of-the-year gift. Students usually received a souvenir card with a photo of the teacher, a list of the students from that year, and the names of the school board members.

After 8 years of attending the one-room school in the country, eighth-grade students would graduate and then attend high school in town. They had 8 years of learning in the country school with all 8 grades together learning from only one teacher.

# School Souvenirs

At the end of the year, the one-room schoolteacher gave each student a special card. Students kept these cards as a way to remember the year.

These stanzas are from a longer poem on a souvenir card given to John Witt, the author's great-uncle, in 1908 by his teacher in Portage County:

*I've labored hard to teach you well,*
*True knowledge to impart,*
*To train the mind in wisdom's ways,*
*And educate the heart.*

*And well I know our coming here*
*For months, from day to day,*
*Has done you good and fitted you*
*To find life's better way.*

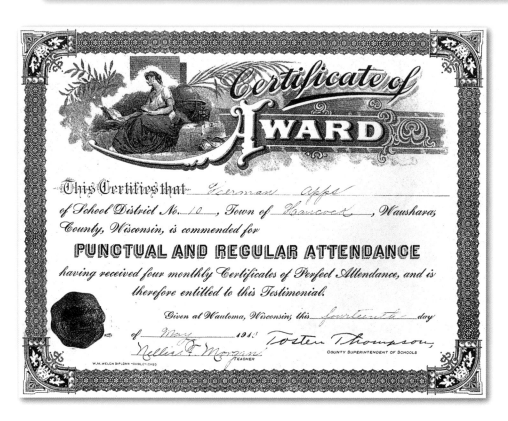

This end-of-the-year attendance award was given to Herman Apps in 1910.
**Collection of Susan Apps-Bodilly**

This former schoolhouse in Paoli is now a shop and restaurant you can visit.

# Chapter 12

## What Happened to the One-Room Schools?

**PAOLI SCHOOLHOUSE**
Shops & Café

**W**isconsin had nearly 6,200 one-room schools in 1938. Why did the one-room schools close? Beginning in the 1940s, some people believed that students in the one-room schools did not receive a good education compared to children who went to school in town. In their opinion, the town schools were better because they were larger and had indoor plumbing and electricity. The school in town had better science equipment, a larger library, a gymnasium, and different teachers for art and music.

Educators from the state who studied **curriculum** also felt that

---

**curriculum** (kuh rik yoo luhm): an organized plan of what will be learned in school

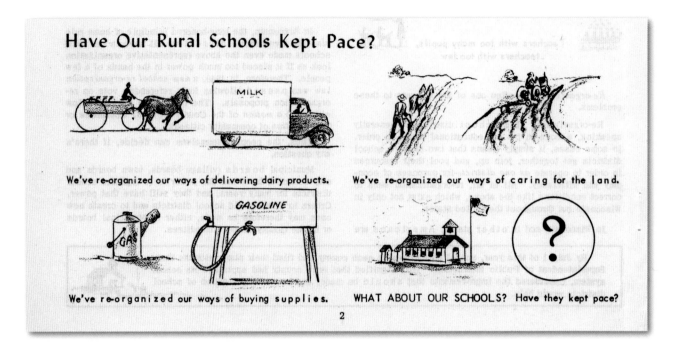

**Have Our Rural Schools Kept Pace?**

MILK

We've re-organized our ways of delivering dairy products.

We've re-organized our ways of caring for the land.

GASOLINE

GAS

We've re-organized our ways of buying supplies.

WHAT ABOUT OUR SCHOOLS? Have they kept pace?

2

This picture from a 1951 publication from the University of Wisconsin Extension Service asks a question about one-room schools. It suggests that rural one-room schools were not meeting the needs of modern life. **WHi Image 86534**

the country school did not provide an **adequate** education for rural children. They did not think that one teacher could provide a quality education in every subject area for all grades. The curriculum that teachers were expected to teach was growing. It was difficult for one teacher to learn the curriculum for all 8 grades.

Also, many older one-room school buildings in Wisconsin needed repair in the 1940s. They needed a new roof or were not warm enough in the winter. Most of the one-room schools were built many years before with no indoor plumbing or electricity. Making repairs to update the buildings would cost a lot of money.

Some parents of rural children agreed with the reasons to close the one-room schools. However, many did not. Those country people felt their schools were successful. Families knew that students from

**adequate** (**ad** uh kwit): good enough

the one-room school did receive an excellent education. Children who attended one-room schools continued on to high school and did very well in their studies. One-room-school students studied and learned together as a **multi-age** group. Bonnie Trudell from the Squaw Lake School in St. Croix County says, "I was the only student in my grade, so I was encouraged to keep learning above my grade. I always had a sense of being able to go at my own speed. From early on, I was assigned an older student to go to if I needed help; if I did not know a word in reading, I had a **mentor** to talk to. I felt like the school belonged to me and my community. Being in a room with kids of all different ages, my brother and sister included, there was a sense of a variety of different needs to be met. I knew that learning was about progress, it is always continuing."

Respect for each other was important at one-room schools, even if a person's background or religion was different. Doing chores and keeping the school running was the job of the teacher, the students, the school board, and the families. Through different social events, the teacher knew the children and their families well. Children and their parents often had grown up going to the same school.

Many schools held meetings to determine if a school would stay open or close. The meetings were difficult. Neighbors often had **opposing viewpoints**. This was a hard time for families. The meetings sometimes created bad feelings among neighbors who were on opposite sides of the issue.

---

**multi-age** (muhl tɪ **ayj**): made up of people of different ages

**mentor** (**men** tuhr): a trusted teacher or adviser

**opposing viewpoints** (uh-**poh**-zing  **vyoo**-points): opinions from opposite sides of an issue

Left: In the early 1950s, many people from the University of Wisconsin did not think the one-room schools were adequate any longer. Information was given out to try to persuade rural parents to agree to close the schools. **WHi Image ID 86533**

Right: This pamphlet from the Wisconsin Rural Schools Association explains that this group was against the closing of one-room schools. **WHi Image ID 86535**

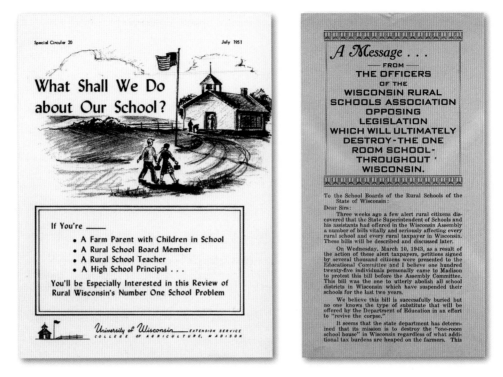

Sometimes an education **expert** from a university attended the meeting. The expert hoped to convince the rural people that closing the school was the right thing to do for the community's children. These experts did not understand the importance of the school as part of the community. They often had not attended a one-room school. They did not understand that closing a country school also meant closing down the center of that neighborhood's community.

In 1939, the Wisconsin State Legislature began to cut funding to rural schools with 10 students or less. Later laws included plans to **consolidate** school districts. By 1962, most Wisconsin students were no longer attending one-room schools.

---

**expert** (**ek** spurt): someone who knows a lot about a topic

**consolidate** (kuhn **sol** uh dayt): join together different parts

After the one-room schools were closed, students went to their new schools on buses. This picture of Janesville students was taken circa 1950. **WHi Image ID 41159**

Even though many people felt that the country schools should stay open, those schools were closed. Students took a bus to school in the closest town. It was the end of an **era** in public education where children and their teacher learned together, almost as a family. Students learned to do their best work independently. Everyone was also expected to help teach others. There was a belief that everyone could learn together, all ages in one room.

The painful closing of a one-room school meant the end of years of gatherings of children and their families. Closing the school took

**era** (**ir** uh): a period of time in history

This brick school building is closed and empty. It is located on Highway 78, south of Blanchardville. The bell has been removed from the bell tower. **Photo by Steve Apps**

away the identity of that community. It destroyed part of what the community was about.

When a school closed, the property was sometimes returned to the original owner and the building was sold or torn down. The desks and contents of the buildings also were sold. But today you can still see many one-room school buildings in the Wisconsin countryside.

Some **former** one-room schools are used now as town halls, homes, gift shops, or restaurants. In the town of Paoli there is a

**former** (**fohr** mur): from before or earlier

building that used to be a schoolhouse. Today it is called the Paoli Schoolhouse Shops & Cafe. This one-room schoolhouse was built in 1854, and a second room was added later. The building was used as a kindergarten classroom until 1972 by the Belleville School District. Today, the building has shops and a restaurant. If you visit there today, you can pull on the long rope of the school bell that hangs in the tower—just as children of the past did to start their school day. Inside, the food "specials of the day" are written on a piece of the chalkboard from the schoolhouse. The building still has the original wood floors that many teachers and children kept clean for years.

The Roger School building and supplies were sold at an auction in 1948 after the school closed. **Courtesy of Jerry Apps**

Some one-room schools are still open as one-room-school museums. You can visit the museum and imagine what it was like to attend school there. When you go, ask yourself if you can smell the soup cooking on the wood stove. Can you hear the reading group sitting with the teacher at the front of the room? Can you see all ages of students working at their desks? Imagine the game of softball in the schoolyard at recess or the families at the picnic on the last day of school.

The Chain O' Lake School had electricity installed in 1944. It did not have a basement, so it never had room for a furnace. The students used the woodstove to keep warm in the winter throughout the years it was open. Faith Jenks was the last teacher at the Chain O' Lake School when it closed in 1955.

Above left: Today the Halfway Prairie School is one of the school museums you can visit around Wisconsin. **Photo by Susan Apps-Bodilly**

Above right: A 1995 view of the Larkin School, which is located in the town of Ogema, Price County. **Courtesy of Jerry Apps**

The Chain O' Lake School still stands as a private home on the same corner in Waushara County. The front gate and the fence are there. The trees that marked the bases for softball are there. The outhouses and flagpole are gone. The front door has been painted red, but it still looks like a one-room schoolhouse.

Today, Darrel Apps, Jerry's younger brother, owns the original clock from the wall of the Chain O' Lake schoolhouse. It hangs on the wall in his home. Sometimes when he hears the tick tock he remembers when he and his classmates were expected to work quietly enough to hear the clock.

Jerry Apps attended the one-room Chain O' Lake School through eighth grade and went on to high school and college. Ruth Olson attended her one-room school in Vernon County through eighth grade, went to high school, and then to college. Jerry met Ruth after college and they got married. They share many stories about their days in one-room schools with their three children and seven grandchildren.

Ask someone older than yourself about what life was like when they were in elementary school. What has changed? What is still the same? What can we learn about teachers and students from schools of the past?

This former schoolhouse in Ripon was built in 1853. It is known as the "Birthplace of the Republican Party." Local citizens who met there on March 20, 1854, decided to form a new political group. You can tour this one-room school building and learn more about its history.
**Courtesy of Ripon Chamber of Commerce**

Children and their teacher play in the Liberty School District #3 schoolyard. This one-room school was located in Grant County.
WHi Image ID 66260

## Appendix I
### Recess Games

**H**ere are some games that students from one-room schoolhouses remember playing. Often, the oldest children were in charge of organizing and leading games while the teacher stayed inside. All ages played together. It was not important to have a winner or a loser at the end of recess. Having fun was the goal. Children also could just run around and roam as long as they could still hear the bell that signaled recess was over. Even though these are games from the past, you can try playing all of these games on your school playground. Get some friends together and have fun. You will feel like a student from a one-room schoolhouse!

## Animal, Vegetable, Mineral

This is a great guessing game also called 20 Questions.

**Materials needed:** none

**How to play:**

*Animal* means any living thing, such as animal, person, or insect, and also anything made from an animal, such as a sweater made of sheep's wool. *Vegetable* means any plant or something made from a plant, such as something made of wood, which comes from a tree. *Mineral* means anything that is not an animal or a plant.

1. One person thinks of an object for everyone else to guess. For example, if the secret thing is a horse, the leader says, "I am thinking of something that is an animal."
2. Other players take turns asking questions. The questions must be answerable with only a "yes" or a "no." Players listen to each other's questions for clues about what to ask next.
3. The leader keeps track of how many questions have been asked.
4. The object of the game is for the guessers to figure out what "it" is in less than 20 questions.

## Anti-I-Over (also called Annie-Over, Aunti-Over)

This was a favorite game for many children at one-room schools. They played it by throwing the ball over a low-roofed building, like the woodshed or the schoolhouse. Today, children could throw the ball over a swing set or part of a piece of playground equipment.

**Materials needed:** a round, bouncy rubber ball and something high to throw it over

**How to play:**

1. Children split up into 2 teams of an even number on opposite sides of the building. One is the "tossing the ball team" and the other is the "catching team."

2. A player from the tossing team throws the ball over the building and yells, "Anti-I-Over!"

3. The ball must bounce on the ground once. The player who is closest to where the ball bounced on the catching team must try to catch the ball. If the player does catch it, then the entire catching team runs around to the tossing team's side of the building.

4. The person who caught the ball tries to tag members of the tossing team, by touching them with the ball or throwing the ball at them. If the ball touches a member of the tossing side, that person joins the catching team.

5. The teams then switch roles and it is the catching team's turn to throw.

6. The purpose of the game is for one side to capture all the players from the other.

### Button, Button, Who's Got the Button?

This game was also good for days when recess took place inside. Some teachers had students try to pass a chalkboard eraser secretly around the circle. This would be a little more difficult to hide!

**Materials needed:** a button

**How to play:**

1. Players stand or sit in a circle.
2. One player is chosen to be "it." Then that person looks away for a bit.
3. One player is chosen by the teacher to hold the button and keep it hidden.
4. The "it" player comes to stand in the center of the circle and says, "Button, button, who's got the button?"
5. Players pass the button around the circle as secretly as they can, while the person who is "it" tries to guess who has the button.
6. If the right person is guessed, this person becomes "it" and the guesser joins the circle.

### Drop the Handkerchief

This game is like Duck, Duck, Goose, but the players carry an object.

**Materials needed:** a clean handkerchief or an eraser

## How to play:

1. Players sit in a circle. One person is chosen to be "it."

2. The person who is "it" walks around the outside of the circle carrying the handkerchief.

3. He/she drops it behind another player and starts to run.

4. The player who has the handkerchief behind then grabs it, gets up, and chases "it" around the circle.

5. The person who is "it" tries to run back to the chosen player's spot and sit down before getting tagged.

6. The player who had to get up and run is "it" if he or she couldn't catch the previous "it" person.

## Fox and Geese

This tag game was played in the winter so tracks could be made in fresh snow. Today, a circle with "spokes" like a wheel could be drawn with chalk on a blacktop surface.

**Materials needed:** none

## How to play:

1. A large circle is tramped in the snow. Then, 2 cross paths are walked out, forming a plus sign through the middle of the circle.

2. One player is the "fox" and all of the others are "geese."

3. The object of the game is to tag all of the geese.

4. The center of the circle, where the paths cross, is a "safe" spot—but only one person can be there at a time.

5. The fox runs around and tries to tag all of the geese.
   Everyone must stay on the path of the circle or the plus-
   sign. Anyone who is tagged by the fox then helps the fox
   tag the rest of the geese.

6. The last goose to be tagged is the next fox.

## Hide the Chalk

This is an inside game for a rainy day.

**Materials needed:** a piece of chalk or a pencil

**How to play:**

1. One player is sent from the room and doesn't peek.

2. The teacher assigns one student to hide the chalk or pencil
   in the room, in plain sight, but in a tricky spot to see. The
   group knows where the object is, but doesn't talk.

3. The finder comes back into the room and starts to search
   for the object.

4. While the finder is looking around, the group claps very
   softly if the finder is not near the object. When the finder
   is near the object, the group claps loudly. The clapping is a
   clue to help the finder in the search.

5. A variation is to have the group say "hot" if the finder is
   very near the object and "cold" or "freezing cold" if the
   finder is far from the object.

## Kick the Can

This game is a fun variation of Hide and Seek.

**Materials needed:** an old can

**How to play:**

1. One person is "it." This person puts the can at "home base."
2. Another player kicks the can as hard as possible in the opposite direction of various hiding spots.
3. The "it" person goes to get the can while all of the others hide. The "it" person puts the can back at home base.
4. While the "it" person tries to find the hiders, he or she must also keep an eye on home base.
5. The hiders try to sneak to home base and kick the can without getting caught by the "it" person. If someone can do this, the player who was "it" must continue to be "it" again. Everyone comes in and the game starts over with new hiding places.
6. When the "it" person does find someone, that person is brought to wait by the can.
7. If the "it" person can find all of the hiding players without anyone kicking the can, that person can choose who is "it" next.

## London Bridge

This is a fun singing game.

**Materials needed:** none

**How to play:**
1. Two children are chosen to be the bridge.
2. These 2 join hands and hold their arms up in the air so the others can walk under.
3. Other children form a line and sing this song:

   *London Bridge is falling down,*
   *Falling down, falling down,*
   *London Bridge is falling down,*
   *My fair lady.*

4. At the words "My fair lady," the children making the bridge drop their arms and the person who is in their arms is "caught."

## Mother May I?

A variation of this game is for the leader to be called "Captain" and the players say, "Captain, may I?"

**Materials needed:** none

**How to play:**

1. One person is the "mother."

2. Everyone else spreads out across the playground but within hearing distance.

3. The "mother" calls out an instruction for everyone, such as, "Take one giant step, "Take one baby step," or "Skip 3 steps" etc. The "mother" can think up anything for the players to do.

4. The players must remember to ask, "Mother may I?"

5. The "mother" answers either, "Yes, you may" or "No, you may not." If she says, "Yes, you may" then everyone does the direction and moves toward the mother.

6. If a player forgets to ask first, or makes a mistake because he or she wasn't following the instruction, that person is out of the game.

7. The first person to reach the "mother" becomes the new "mother."

## Passing Relay Races

Relay races were played inside, along a row of desks, or outside at community picnics. Teachers made up many variations of relay races.

**Materials needed:** something to pass along a line of children, such as a ruler, piece of fruit, a hat, or a book

**How to play:**

1. Children are divided into even lines standing or sitting facing the same direction.

2. When the teacher or leader gives the signal to begin, the first player, or the "captain," in each line picks up the object in his or her right hand and quickly passes it back over the left shoulder to the next person in line. The passer cannot turn around.

3. The next person in line continues passing the object back until it reaches the last person in the row.

4. The last person taps the person in front him on his right shoulder and passes the object back up the row as quickly as possible without dropping it on the floor. When the object reaches the "captain," that person stands up so the teacher knows that row is done first.

## Red Rover

This is a fun game for a large group of children.

**Materials needed:** none

**How to play:**

1. Two lines of students stand across a field from each other.

2. One player is chosen to be "it." This person stands in the center of the field.

3. "It" calls out, "Red Rover, Red Rover, let _____ (child's name) come over."

4.  The person who is named attempts to run across the field without getting tagged by the "it" person in the middle. If the runner is tagged, then that person joins the "it" person in the middle. He or she helps tag the next runner who is called to run through.

Above: Today, you can visit the Raspberry School at Old World Wisconsin. A guide will answer your questions about being a student in this one-room school. **Wisconsin Historical Society**. Far right: A scene of people gathering outside the Raspberry School in 1906. The one-room schoolhouse was built in Bayfield County in northern Wisconsin in 1896. **WHi Image ID 39538**

# Appendix II

## Visit a One-Room Schoolhouse

On the pages that follow is a selection of one-room schools around the state that you can tour. Check with your local historical society for information about other one-room schools in your area.

## Barron County: Joliet School at Pioneer Village Museum

The Joliet School was located in the township of Stanley on the west side of the Red Cedar River. Gus Benson sold one acre of his farm for the school, which was built in 1905. In the early days, there was no bridge to cross the river. Later, a hanging bridge that was one or 2 planks wide was built so children could who lived across the river could get to school. The school closed in 1962, and the building was given to the Barron County Historical Society. The building was moved to the site of Pioneer Village in 1964.

The village has 37 buildings including a town hall, general store, doctor's office, and post office. There is also a farmstead with log buildings.

### Pioneer Village Museum
- 1866 13½–14th Avenue, Cameron
- Open Memorial Day to Labor Day, Thursday through Sunday, 1:00–5:00 p.m. Open in May for school field trips and on other days by appointment.
- (715) 458-2080, www.barroncountymuseum.com

## Burnett County: Karlsborg School at Forts Folle Avoine Historical Park

The Karlsborg School was built in 1887. It was donated to the Burnett County Historical Society and moved to the Forts Folle Avoine site in 2000. The building contains the school's original teacher desk and chair.

The Forts Folle Avoine Historical Park also has an authentic 1802 trading post and a re-created Woodland Indian village depicting the relationship between fur traders and Native Americans. Guides dressed in period clothing lead tours.

### Forts Folle Avoine Historical Park

- 8500 County Road U, Danbury
- Open May to Labor Day, Wednesday through Sunday, 10:00 a.m.–4:00 p.m. Tours for school groups are available.
- (715) 866-8890, http://theforts.org

## Clark County: Reed School, a Wisconsin Historic Site

The Reed School is owned and operated by the Wisconsin Historical Society. It served as a one-room school from 1915 to 1951. Gordon Smith from Gary, Indiana, was sent to Wisconsin by his parents in the spring of 1939. He attended Reed School with his cousins as a first-grader in 1939. After that school year, he returned home to his family. When he was older, he went to Harvard University and became a lawyer. In later life, Mr. Smith felt that he had learned more about responsibility and honesty from his experience at Reed School than at any other time in his life. As an adult, he found out that Reed School was for sale. His organization, the Gordon V. and Helen C. Smith Foundation of Potomac, Maryland, purchased, restored, and provided money to maintain Reed School. The foundation donated the school to the Wisconsin Historical Society in 2007.

School groups that visit the Reed School experience learning as if they lived in the year 1939. They are encouraged to participate, think, and imagine being a student in the school. They learn about the daily lives of children at the end of the Great Depression in rural Wisconsin. An extensive teachers' guide of pre-visit activities, follow-up activities, and other educational materials are available online.

### Reed School

- US Highway 10 & Cardinal Avenue, Neillsville
- Open May to October, Saturday and Sunday, 10:00 a.m.–4:00 p.m. Group tours are available by appointment.
- (608) 253-3523, http://reedschool.wisconsinhistory.org

## Dane County: Halfway Prairie School, part of the Dane County Parks system

Halfway Prairie School is Dane County's oldest rural elementary school. It served the children of local farmers and miners from 1855 to 1961. It was given the name Halfway because it was located halfway between Mineral Point and Portage. This was a route traveled by early Wisconsin miners who camped nearby. Today, the school is part of a small public park. Inside, there are desks, books, and many artifacts representing school life from the 1930s. Visitors can also see outhouses and a hand-crank water pump. Since 1967, the Friends Group of Old Halfway Prairie has restored and maintained the museum. This one-room school is located in the town of Mazomanie at the junction of Highway F and Highway 19.

### Halfway Prairie School

- 9770 Highway 19, Waunakee

- Open May to Labor Day, Sunday, 1:00–5:00 p.m. School tours are available by appointment.
- www.countyofdane.com/lwrd/parks/halfway.aspx

## Grant County: School at Stonefield, a Wisconsin Historic Site

The re-created rural farming village at this Wisconsin Historic Site includes a one-room schoolhouse built in 1897 for Muddy Hollow, town of Cassville school district #4 in Grant County. It closed in 1952. Funds for moving the structure to Stonefield were provided by the Wisconsin Education Association. The village also has a broom-making shop, carpenter shop, and blacksmith shop. At this historic site you can also see tractors, reapers, and threshing machines. Stonefield includes the summer estate of Wisconsin's first governor, Nelson Dewey. Stonefield is located near the Mississippi River along the Great River Road.

### Stonefield
- 12195 Highway VV, Cassville
- Open May to October, daily, 10:00 a.m.–4:00 p.m.
- (608) 725-5210, http://stonefield.wisconsinhistory.org

## Oneida County: Rhinelander School Museum at the Pioneer Park Historical Complex

The Rhinelander School Museum is part of the Pioneer Park Historical Complex. The school was built around 1900 in the township of Newbold and was called the Newhaus School. Later, it was called the Tom Doyle School. It was moved to the town of Pine Lake and called Pine Lake School #2 until 1953. In 1975, many individuals purchased the building and moved it to Pioneer Park for restoration. It opened to the public in 1978. Inside, there are many artifacts from one-room schools. Volunteers are available to answer questions and tell stories about life in a one-room school.

This historical complex also includes the Logging Museum with a re-created 1870s lumberjack camp, a Soo Line depot, railroad facts and displays, a Civilian Conservation Corps Museum, and the Antique Outboard Motor and Fishing Museum.

### Pioneer Park Historical Complex

- Business Highway 8 & Oneida Avenue, Rhinelander
- Open Memorial Day to Labor Day, daily, 10:00 a.m.–5:00 p.m.
- (715) 369-5004, www.explorerhinelander.com/pioneer-park-historical-complex

## Ozaukee County: Stony Hill School, 5595 Highway I, Town of Fredonia

During the 2-hour experience at the Stony Hill School, "teacher" re-creates a school day from the year 1880. A teachers' guide is available. Dates can be scheduled from May until mid-June and from Labor Day to mid-October.

The Stony Hill School is about 2 miles from the Ozaukee County Pioneer Village. The village is a collection of more than 20 buildings and structures from the 1840s to the early 1900s. There are fully

furnished barns and outbuildings, plus the original Cedarburg
Railroad Depot. Start your tour at the village.

### Ozaukee County Pioneer Village

- 4880 County Highway I, Town of Saukville
- Open May to October, Saturday and Sunday, noon–5:00 p.m.
- (262) 377-4510, www.co.ozaukee.wi.us/ochs/PioneerVillage.htm

## St. Croix County: 1902 Camp 9 School at the New Richmond Heritage Center

This school was built in 1902 for the children of Logging Camp 9. It
was moved from its original site near Glenwood City. The heritage
center also has the school's outhouse and a log cabin, blacksmith
shop, barn, granary, general store, and an 1884 farmhouse. A
scavenger hunt tour is offered.

### New Richmond Heritage Center

- 1100 Heritage Drive, New Richmond
- Open year-round, Monday to Friday, 10:00 a.m.–4:00 p.m.
- (715) 246-3276, www.nrheritagecenter.org

## Waukesha County: Raspberry School at Old World Wisconsin, a Wisconsin Historic Site

The Raspberry School was built in 1896 by 3 Scandinavian families in
Bayfield County. It was named for Raspberry Bay in Lake Superior.
The school was moved to the Old World Wisconsin site at Eagle

and restored to its 1906 appearance. The school is located in the Norwegian area. A volunteer "schoolmaster" re-creates the experience of a one-room school.

Old World Wisconsin is an outdoor museum featuring demonstrations of nineteenth-century immigrant farm and rural life. Interpreters dressed in period clothing work in the Danish, Finnish, German, Irish, Norwegian, Polish, and Yankee areas. Craftspeople work in the 1870s Crossroads Village. A chapel and church are in the African American area. Historically accurate heirloom gardens of grains, fruits, and vegetables are also tended by interpreters in period dress. Visitors can also see historic breeds of farm animals.

### Old World Wisconsin

- W372 S9727 Highway 67, Eagle
- Open May to October, daily. Check the museum website for hours.
- (262) 594-630, http://oldworldwisconsin.wisconsinhistory.org

## Waushara County: Progressive School at the Wild Rose Pioneer Museum

The Progressive School was also known as Swamp School. It was built in 1894 and moved to its present site by the Waushara County Retired Teachers Association in 1983. The group then constructed a new foundation, replaced interior walls, and built a new chimney. Some members located the original school bell. They also collected books and furnishings for the building. Today, retired teachers are tour guides in the school. The Wild Rose Pioneer Museum complex grounds also include the 1880 Elisha Stewart House and a barn, blacksmith shop, smokehouse, and carriage house.

### Wild Rose Pioneer Museum

- Highway 22/Main Street, Wild Rose
- Open mid-June to Labor Day, Wednesday and Saturday, 1:00–4:00 p.m.
- (608) 833-2782, www.1wisconsin.com/wildrose/Museum/museum.htm

| | |
|---|---|
| a | c<u>a</u>t (kat), pl<u>ai</u>d (plad), h<u>a</u>lf (haf) |
| ah | f<u>a</u>ther (**fah** THur), h<u>ea</u>rt (hahrt) |
| air | c<u>a</u>rry (**kair** ee), b<u>ear</u> (bair), wh<u>ere</u> (whair) |
| aw | <u>a</u>ll (awl), l<u>aw</u> (law), b<u>ough</u>t (bawt) |
| ay | s<u>ay</u> (say), br<u>ea</u>k (brayk), v<u>ei</u>n (vayn) |
| e | b<u>e</u>t (bet), s<u>ay</u>s (sez), d<u>ea</u>f (def) |
| ee | b<u>ee</u> (bee), t<u>ea</u>m (teem), f<u>ea</u>r (feer) |
| i | b<u>i</u>t (bit), w<u>o</u>men (**wim** uhn), b<u>ui</u>ld (bild) |
| ɪ | <u>i</u>ce (ɪs), l<u>ie</u> (lɪ), sk<u>y</u> (skɪ) |
| o | h<u>o</u>t (hot), w<u>a</u>tch (wotch) |
| oh | <u>o</u>pen (**oh** puhn), s<u>ew</u> (soh) |
| oi | b<u>oi</u>l (boil), b<u>oy</u> (boi) |
| oo | p<u>oo</u>l (pool), m<u>o</u>ve (moov), sh<u>oe</u> (shoo) |
| or | <u>or</u>der (**or** dur), m<u>ore</u> (mor) |
| ou | h<u>ou</u>se (hous), n<u>ow</u> (nou) |
| u | g<u>oo</u>d (gud), sh<u>ou</u>ld (shud) |
| uh | c<u>u</u>p (kuhp), fl<u>oo</u>d (fluhd), butt<u>o</u>n (**buht** uhn) |
| ur | b<u>ur</u>n (burn), p<u>ear</u>l (purl), b<u>ir</u>d (burd) |
| yoo | <u>u</u>se (yooz), f<u>ew</u> (fyoo), v<u>iew</u> (vyoo) |
| hw | <u>wh</u>at (hwuht), <u>wh</u>en (hwen) |
| TH | <u>th</u>at (THat), brea<u>the</u> (breeTH) |
| zh | mea<u>s</u>ure (**mezh** ur), gara<u>ge</u> (guh **razh**) |

# Glossary

**adequate** (**ad** uh kwit): good enough

**armistice** (**ahr** muh stis): an agreement between enemy countries to stop a war

**assist** (uh **sist**): to provide help

**blustery** (**bluhs** tur ee): having stormy weather with strong wind

**candidate** (**kan** duh dayt): someone running for office in an election

**cease-fire** (**sees** fir): the end of the fighting of a war

**citizen** (**sit** uh zuhn): member of a particular country who has the right to live there

**consolidate** (kuhn **sol** uh dayt): join together different parts

**cooperation** (koh op uh **ray** shuhn): working together to reach a goal

**curriculum** (kuh **rik** yoo luhm): an organized plan of what will be learned in school

**dawdler** (**dawd** lur): someone who wastes time or takes a long time to do something

**demoted** (di **moh** tid): sent down to a lower job or rank

**emigrated** (**em** uh gray tid): left one's own country to settle in another

**era** (**ir** uh): a period of time in history

**ethnic group** (eth **nik** group): a group of people sharing the same home country or culture

**evaporate** (i **vap** uh rayt): change into vapor and become part of the air

**exchanged** (eks **chaynjd**): gave one thing for another

**expectation** (ek spek **tay** shun): an idea or belief about what should happen

**expert** (**ek** spurt): someone who knows a lot about a topic

**finale** (fuh **nal** ee): the last part of a performance or show

**former** (**fohr** mur): from before or earlier

**historian** (hi **stor** ee uhn): someone who studies and tells or writes about the past

**influenced** (**in** floo uhnsd): affected someone or something

**lard** (lahrd): white grease used for cooking, made from melted fat

**license** (lɪ suhns): a document showing permission or approval from the government

**mentor** (**men** tuhr): a trusted teacher or adviser

**multi-age** (muhl tɪ **ayj**): made up of people of different ages

**normal school** (**nor**-muhl skool): a 2-year school for training teachers

**observe** (uhb **zurv**): celebrate a holiday

**opposing viewpoints** (uh-**poh**-zing **vyoo**-points): opinions from opposite sides of an issue

**pasteurized** (**pas** chuh rɪzd): the state of milk after it has been heated to a high temperature to kill harmful bacteria

**patriotic** (pay tree **ot** ik): showing love and loyalty for one's country

**pint jar** (pɪnt jahr): a jar that can hold 16 fluid ounces

**responsible** (ri **spon** suh buhl): having important duties, being in charge

**qualification** (kwahl uh fuh **kay** shuhn): a skill that makes you able to do a task

**quartet** (kwor **tet**): a group of 4 people playing music or singing together

**recitation** (res i **tay** shuhn): a speech that is memorized and performed

**recite** (ri **sɪt**): say something aloud that you have memorized

**requirement** (ri **kwɪr** muhnt): something that you have to do

**rural** (**rur** uhl): having to do with the countryside or farming

**sawhorse** (**saw** hors): a stand used to support pieces of wood that are being sawed

**silhouette** (sil oo **et**): a dark outline visible against a light background

**solo** (**soh** loh): part of a song performed by one person

**superintendent** (soo pur in **ten** duhnt): the person in charge of a school system

**suspenders** (suh **spen** durz): straps worn over a person's shoulders and attached to their pants to hold them up

**tablet** (**tab** lit): a pad of paper stuck together on one end and used for writing

**unexpectedly** (uhn ek **spek** tid lee): happening without warning

**unseemly** (uhn **seem** lee): not in good taste or judgment

**versus** (**vur** suhs): against

**Wisconsin Idea** (wi-**skon**-suhn ɪ-**dee**-uh): the goal that knowledge and developments from the University of Wisconsin will be used to benefit those living in the state

# Acknowledgments

As I tell my students, many people help to write a book. I gratefully acknowledge Kathy Borkowski, Bobbie Malone, Barbara Walsh, Laura Kearney, Diane Drexler, and Shaun Miller from the Wisconsin Historical Society Press. Thank you to Virginia Hanson and Mary Ann DeVries of the Madison Metropolitan School District and the students who read and commented on the recess and lunch chapters. Thank you to the volunteers at the Rhinelander School Museum at the Pioneer Park Historical Complex, especially Lily (Wolff) Kongslien. Thank you to many former teachers and students from one-room schools who so willingly described their memories of this special time, especially Darlene Jacobson Ingrassia. Thank you to my brother, Steve Apps, for his photography. Special thanks to my parents, Jerry and Ruth Apps, for sharing their stories for this book. There are many memories from my Aunt Marilyn and Uncle Darrel, and Aunt Marcie and Uncle Donald, who attended one-room schools and shared their stories for this project. Thank you to my father for use of the research he collected for his book, *One-Room Country Schools: History and Recollections*. I would like to thank my Grandpa and Grandma Apps for saving school report cards, pictures, end-of-the-year souvenir cards, and the Chain O' Lake treasurer's book. These special primary-source materials make your stories come alive many years later.

Opposite: The Reed School in Neillsville is now a Wisconsin Historic Site. Classes were taught in this one-room school from 1915 to 1951. Photo by Mark Fay

PUBLIC SCHOOL, BRIDGE

Clockwise from top left: Teacher and students stand outside of their log schoolhouse in Weston, 1897. **WHi Image ID 29420.** The children stand in neat rows outside a Watertown schoolhouse. Many of the students are not wearing shoes. **WHi Image ID 66098.** A group of students pose for a picture on the fence in front of the Fennimore District #7 school building. **WHi Image ID 66234.** A Fennimore District class shown outside their school building. **WHi Image ID 66222.** In Bridgeport, students and their teacher pose outside in winter for a photo. **WHi Image ID 84689.** Children pose in front of Hillcrest School in Waukesha County, circa 1933. Did you notice the bell tower and chimney? **WHi Image ID 86209**

# Index

This index points you to the pages where you can read about persons, places, and ideas. If you do not find the word you are looking for, try to think of another word that means about the same thing.

When you see a page number in **bold** it means there is a picture on that page.

# About the Author

**S**usan Apps-Bodilly has been an elementary and middle-school teacher for more than 20 years. She currently teaches second- and third-grade students. She has a master's degree in Curriculum and Instruction from the University of Wisconsin–Madison and holds a reading teacher license. When she is not teaching, reading, or writing, she loves to spend time biking or hiking in the woods with her family. She has a longtime interest in history and a passion for engaging children in learning about today from stories of the past. She has a daughter and son-in-law in Minneapolis and lives in Madison with her husband and 3 sons.

**Photo by Steve Apps**